America's Founding Fathers

ALEXANDER HAMILTON

Creating a Nation

Zachary Kent

Enslow Publishers, Inc.

40 Industrial Road	PO Box 38
Box 398	Aldershot
Berkeley Heights, NJ 07922	Hants GU12 6BP
USA	UK

http://www.enslow.com

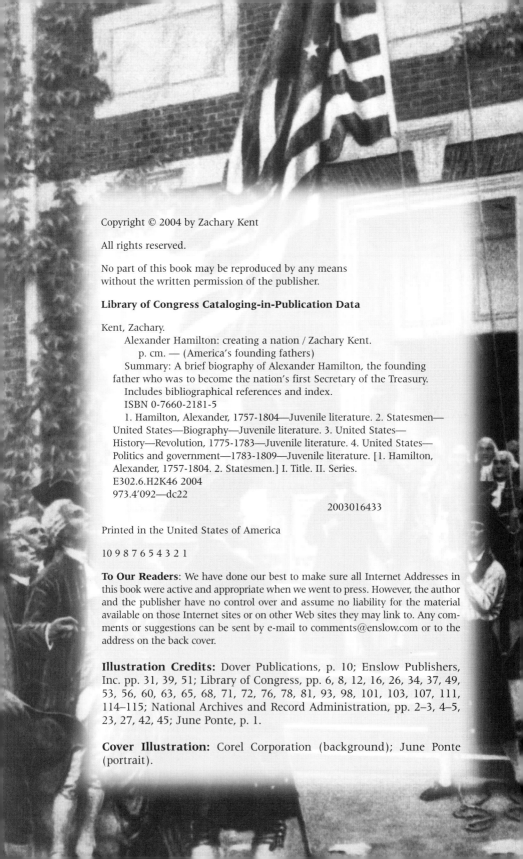

Library of Congress Cataloging-in-Publication Data

Kent, Zachary.
    Alexander Hamilton: creating a nation / Zachary Kent.
        p. cm. — (America's founding fathers)
    Summary: A brief biography of Alexander Hamilton, the founding
father who was to become the nation's first Secretary of the Treasury.
    Includes bibliographical references and index.
    ISBN 0-7660-2181-5
    1. Hamilton, Alexander, 1757-1804—Juvenile literature. 2. Statesmen—
United States—Biography—Juvenile literature. 3. United States—
History—Revolution, 1775-1783—Juvenile literature. 4. United States—
Politics and government—1783-1809—Juvenile literature. [1. Hamilton,
Alexander, 1757-1804. 2. Statesmen.] I. Title. II. Series.
E302.6.H2K46 2004
973.4'092—dc22

                                                    2003016433

Printed in the United States of America

10 9 8 7 6 5 4 3 2 1

To Our Readers: We have done our best to make sure all Internet Addresses in
this book were active and appropriate when we went to press. However, the author
and the publisher have no control over and assume no liability for the material
available on those Internet sites or on other Web sites they may link to. Any com-
ments or suggestions can be sent by e-mail to comments@enslow.com or to the
address on the back cover.

Illustration Credits: Dover Publications, p. 10; Enslow Publishers,
Inc. pp. 31, 39, 51; Library of Congress, pp. 6, 8, 12, 16, 26, 34, 37, 49,
53, 56, 60, 63, 65, 68, 71, 72, 76, 78, 81, 93, 98, 101, 103, 107, 111,
114–115; National Archives and Record Administration, pp. 2–3, 4–5,
23, 27, 42, 45; June Ponte, p. 1.

Cover Illustration: Corel Corporation (background); June Ponte
(portrait).

*C*ontents

The Declaration of Independence was adopted in 1776. A few years later states would ratify a new document—the Constitution.

The Fight for the Constitution

AT THE END OF THE Revolutionary War in 1783, the United States won its independence from Great Britain. In 1787, delegates from twelve of the thirteen states met in Philadelphia. Together, they designed a strong new government for the nation. The set of laws they wrote was called the Constitution. The delegates decided that at least nine of the thirteen states must agree to the Constitution for it to go into effect. By June 1788, eight states had voted to ratify: Delaware, Pennsylvania, New Jersey, Georgia, Connecticut, Massachusetts, Maryland, and South Carolina. One more state was needed.

In the summer of 1788, a slender man with reddish brown hair and violet blue eyes stood at the state ratification convention in Poughkeepsie, New York. "The establishment of a republican government," he addressed his fellow delegates, "is . . . nearest and dearest to my own heart. . . . The true principle of a republic is that the people should choose whom they please to govern them."[1] This man was thirty-three-year-old Alexander Hamilton.

Alexander Hamilton worked hard to persuade New Yorkers to ratify the Constitution. He believed the United States would not survive without a strong national government.

The Importance of New York

New York was one of the largest of the thirteen states in both size and population. Many Americans believed that the success of the Constitution depended on whether New York ratified the document. Without New York, the nation would be geographically cut in two, and the future of the entire United States could easily be ruined.

New Yorkers who were against the Constitution had won forty-six seats to the state ratification convention in 1788. New Yorkers in favor of the document had only won nineteen seats. It seemed certain the Constitution would be voted down in New York.

The New York convention assembled on June 17, 1788, in the Poughkeepsie courthouse. Robert R. Livingston, James Duane, John Jay, and Alexander Hamilton were among the delegates strongly in favor of ratification. Governor George Clinton, John Lansing, Jr., Charles Tillinghast, and Melancton Smith led those delegates against the Constitution. They distrusted a strong national government. Clinton especially feared that the Constitution would weaken his political power in the state.

On June 24, word arrived that New Hampshire had become the ninth state to ratify. The Constitution was adopted, even though New York had not yet made its decision. But many people still believed the United States could not succeed if New York refused to ratify.

Hamilton Speaks Out

Hamilton addressed the convention day after day. He discussed the Constitution in detail. "When you have divided and nicely balanced the departments of government," he exclaimed, ". . . when, in short, you have rendered your system as perfect as human forms can be;—you must place confidence; you must give power."[2] One witness remarked that Hamilton made "powerful appeals to the moral sense and patriotism, the fears and hopes of the assembly."[3] Hamilton reminded delegates that New York's state government in fact was very much like the national government outlined in the Constitution. Both governments had two legislative chambers, a strong executive, and the power to tax people.

On July 2, a messenger galloped on horseback to the courthouse door and delivered a letter for Hamilton. It was the thrilling news that Virginia had voted to ratify the Constitution. When Poughkeepsie citizens heard the news, they began marching outside the courthouse in happy celebration. Virginia's decision had a great effect on New York delegates. Virginia was the largest and most populated of the thirteen states. Several New York delegates now changed their minds. They announced their support for the Constitution.

On July 15, Melancton Smith suggested that the convention ratify the Constitution. But he insisted that the state be allowed to change its decision unless certain amendments to the Constitution were later adopted. Hamilton wrote to Virginian James Madison asking if such a condition would be acceptable. Madison's reputation as a Constitution scholar was widely respected. Madison quickly wrote back. He thought Smith's request that New York have "a right to withdraw, if amendments be not decided on, [would not make the state] a member of the new Union."[4]

In a dramatic speech, Hamilton demanded that the delegates finally accept

This is a portrait of James Madison. While Hamilton fought to get the Constitution ratified in New York, Madison did the same in Virginia. Having studied the subject for years, no one knew more about constitutional law than Madison did.

the Constitution or reject it. If they wanted, they could send a list of recommended amendments along with the ratified document. A witness recalled the force of Hamilton's arguments. He thought Hamilton was like a "political porcupine, armed at all points."[5]

In the end, his arguments convinced Melancton Smith. On July 24, Smith suddenly stood and announced he would drop his demand for amendments. He would now vote to ratify. Other delegates also changed their minds. On July 26, the delegates finally voted. By a close vote of 30 to 25, New York decided to support the Constitution.

A Grand Parade

Three days earlier, citizens in New York City had already guessed how the vote would go. They celebrated the new Constitution with a grand parade down Broadway. Leading the parade was a giant float pulled by ten horses. It was the twenty-seven-foot model of a ship named the *Hamilton*.

A banner in the parade exclaimed, "Behold the federal ship of fame; The *Hamilton* we call her name."[6]

Most New Yorkers recognized that Alexander Hamilton had won ratification of the Constitution in their state. The model ship *Hamilton* was their way of honoring him.

At ten o'clock on the morning of July 23, thirteen guns were fired from the *Hamilton*. It was the signal for the parade to begin. The float rolled forward. It made "a fine appearance," declared one newspaper,

New Yorkers celebrated the new Constitution with a parade.

"sailing with flowing sheets and full sails, down Broadway . . . "[7] Thousands of cheering people crowded the sidewalks to watch it pass. One marcher in the parade took special pride. Sixteen years earlier, American businessman Nicholas Cruger had owned an import-export company on the Caribbean island of St. Croix. With a generous heart, Cruger had helped pay to send his young clerk, Alexander Hamilton, to America for a college education.

The Founding Fathers

Alexander Hamilton belongs to a special group of Americans. They are remembered today as the founding fathers. During the 1770s and 1780s, the founding fathers created a new and independent nation, the United States of America. The creation of the United States was truly remarkable. It was a revolution, in fact. It seemed to turn the entire world upside down. It marked a complete and surprisingly successful change in the country's government.

Boyhood in the West Indies

ALEXANDER HAMILTON was born on January 11, 1757, in the town of Charlestown, on the small island of Nevis. Nevis is one of the Caribbean Islands. It is located in what was called the British West Indies. These were a string of islands claimed and settled by Great Britain as colonies in the 1700s.

An Unhappy Marriage

Hamilton's mother, Rachel Faucett, had been born on Nevis and had grown up on the Caribbean island of St. Croix. St. Croix was a colonial island of Denmark. (Today it is part of the Virgin Islands.) Its capital was the town of Christiansted. In February 1745, Rachel's mother wanted her to marry John Lavien. Lavien was many years older than Rachel, who was only sixteen years old. He was a shopkeeper and owned a share in a St. Croix cotton plantation. Rachel did not love him. But her mother believed that her daughter would gain a comfortable life by marrying him.[1]

In 1746, Rachel Faucett Lavien gave birth to a baby boy, Peter. But her married life was unhappy. In 1750, Lavien entered the office of the town captain of Christiansted. "I want you to jail my wife!" he insisted.[2] He claimed that Rachel refused to live with him anymore. He filed a complaint charging that his wife had "twice been guilty of adultery."[3] Rachel was soon arrested and locked in a cell in the fort in Christiansted Harbor. When Lavien finally agreed to let her out of jail, she ran away, abandoning Lavien and her four-year-old son. Rachel left St. Croix in October 1750.

James Hamilton

It is uncertain where Rachel Faucett Lavien met James Hamilton. It may have been on the island of Nevis.[4] Hamilton was the fourth son of Alexander Hamilton, a British nobleman, and the Laird of

It is believed Alexander Hamilton was born in the town of Charlestown on the Caribbean island of Nevis. Some scholars still argue about when and where Hamilton was born because no official record of his birth was kept.

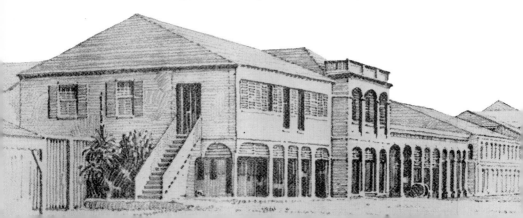

Cambuskeith in Ayrshire, Scotland. As a younger son, James Hamilton knew he would not inherit his father's title. That would go to the oldest son. Hamilton had journeyed to the British West Indies hoping to become rich as a merchant. Around 1752, Rachel Faucett Lavien began living with Hamilton. However, she had not gotten a divorce from John Lavien. She and Hamilton had their first child, James, Jr., in 1753. Two years later, Alexander was born.

In time, John Lavien learned that his wife and James Hamilton were living together. He realized she would never return to him. In the spring of 1759, Lavien appeared before the governor of St. Croix and five judges. In divorce papers, he charged Rachel with being "shameless, rude and ungodly." She had, he claimed, "completely forgotten her duty and let husband and child alone."[5] The court granted Lavien a divorce. According to Danish law, Lavien could marry again, and he did. But Rachel was not allowed to remarry under the law.

Failed Hopes

James Hamilton never fulfilled his dreams of success. In the Caribbean Islands, he found work where he could, often earning a poor living as an office clerk. Years later, Alexander recalled that his father, "became bankrupt as a merchant at an early day in the West Indies. . . . My heart bleeds at the recollection" of his "misfortunes and embarrassments."[6]

Traveling from job to job, the Hamilton family finally arrived on the British island of St. Kitts.

Hamilton found work as chief clerk for a merchant named Charles Ingram. In 1765, Ingram ordered his clerk to journey to Christiansted, St. Croix, to collect a debt. It would take some time to make the full collection. Hamilton took Rachel and their two sons with him.

In 1766, Hamilton sailed back to St. Kitts on business. He never returned to his family, who remained on St. Croix. It is unclear why he abandoned his wife and children. Alexander Hamilton would later explain, "My father's affairs at a very early date went to wreck. . . . This state of things occasioned a separation between him and me, when I was very young . . . "[7] Alexander wrote to his father as he grew older. They seemed to continue a loving, distant relationship. James Hamilton lived a long and uneventful life in the Caribbean Islands. In 1799, he died an old man. Of his father's life, Alexander Hamilton would write that he had "too much pride" and not enough ambition to become a success.[8]

Alone in the World

To support herself and her two young sons, Rachel opened a general store in Christiansted. Two business partners, David Beekman and Nicholas Cruger, ran an import-export company at the lower end of King Street. They sold her imported goods to sell in her store. She kept two sheds in the rear. There, young Alexander helped stack and count barrels of salted pork and fish and bags of flour and rice.

"Alex," as he was called, spent little time in school. His mother and Grandmother Faucett taught him

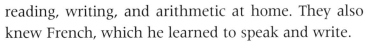

reading, writing, and arithmetic at home. They also knew French, which he learned to speak and write.

In February 1768, Alex and his mother both fell ill with fever. Although the boy slowly recovered, his mother died on February 19, 1768, at the age of thirty-nine. After her death, it had to be decided how her possessions would be divided. The most valuable items included thirteen silver spoons and thirty-four books. Alexander and his brother James hoped to inherit what their mother had worked so hard to gain. But John Lavien appeared in court. Lavien claimed the entire inheritance for his son Peter. Peter was, he pointed out, Rachel's only legal son, because she and James Hamilton had never married. In the end, the court agreed. The Hamilton brothers received nothing.

At the age of thirteen, Alex had to go to work to survive. His brother James became the apprentice to a carpenter named Thomas McNobeny. Alex found a job as a clerk for Nicholas Cruger.

The Skilled Clerk

Cruger was now in business for himself. He imported such products as lumber, cattle, and food from the American colonies. From St. Croix, he exported sugar, molasses, and rum. Cruger also bought and sold slaves in the Christiansted slave market. He owned ships, warehouses, a general store, and a loan office.

Alex proved a bright and eager clerk. He assisted Cruger in making business arrangements with merchants, planters, sea captains, lawyers, and government officials. He later remembered his work at Cruger's "as the most useful part of [my] education."[9]

By 1771, Alex had become Cruger's senior clerk. He sat at a desk writing in Cruger's account books. He prepared contracts and wrote business letters. In November of that year, Cruger fell ill. The businessman decided to make a long visit to relatives in New York City in the colony of New York to improve his health. Boarding a ship for the voyage, Cruger left his senior clerk Hamilton in charge. For the next six months, Alex ran Cruger's entire business. The "young man," as Cruger called him, was only sixteen years old.[10]

This portrait of Hamilton was drawn in 1773 on his eighteenth birthday. At that age, he still looked like a young boy. But Hamilton had already shown he was skilled enough to run Nicholas Cruger's entire import-export company.

Alex was not afraid of his great responsibility. He immediately took control and ran the company skillfully. He wrote letters to New York City, to keep his boss informed. "I think he seems to lack experience in such voyages," he commented on one of the company's ship captains in a letter to Cruger.[11] In another letter, he gave his opinion that one of Cruger's ships was "not so swift as she ought to be."[12]

During his time in charge, Alex boldly fired the company's lawyer and hired another. When Nicholas Cruger finally returned to St. Croix in March 1772, he found his business running smoothly.

A Golden Opportunity

In 1771, the Reverend Hugh Knox landed at Christiansted. He took up the work of a Presbyterian minister on St. Croix. Knox soon became a friend of Alexander Hamilton. He quickly grew to like the hard-working young clerk. Knox owned a collection of books, which he allowed Hamilton to read. Together, they discussed their readings. Knox soon realized that Hamilton had an eager and uncommon mind.

On August 31, 1772, a hurricane struck St. Croix. Giant waves sent harbor boats crashing onto the shore. Raging winds tore trees up from their roots. Thirty people died in the awful storm. Afterwards, Hamilton penned a letter to his father describing the event. "Good God! what horror and destruction," he exclaimed.[13]

Before sending the letter, Hamilton showed it to Knox. Amazed at how well written the letter was, Knox sent it to a local newspaper where it was published. Many St. Croix citizens admitted Hamilton was an especially intelligent young man. It was then that Knox suggested that Hamilton should be sent to America to attend college. In those days, neighbors sometimes helped deserving people in this way. Knox, Cruger, as well as other St. Croix merchants, took up a collection. They gathered enough money to provide

The roaring of the sea and wind . . . the prodigious glare of almost perpetual lightning . . . were sufficient to strike astonishment into Angels. A great part of the buildings throughout the Island are leveled to the ground . . . whole families running about the streets unknowing where to find a place of shelter—the sick . . . without a bed to lie upon—or a dry covering to their bodies—our harbor is entirely bare.[14]

Hamilton's letter describing the hurricane that struck St. Croix in August 1772 was full of exciting detail.

Hamilton with an opportunity to improve himself. Years later, Knox would tell him, "I have always had a just and secret pride in having advised you to go to America . . ."[15] Alexander Hamilton was about to begin a grand adventure. It would change his life and, in time, the history of the United States.

Young Revolutionary

AT THE END of September 1772, seventeen-year-old Alexander Hamilton boarded a ship and journeyed northward. After a three-week voyage, the ship docked in Boston, Massachusetts, on October 22. At once, Hamilton set out by stagecoach for New York City. To a young man used to St. Croix and small island life, New York City was impressive. Some twenty-five thousand people walked its busy streets in 1772.

The young man presented himself to businessman Cornelius Kortright. Rev. Hugh Knox had sent money for Hamilton's support to his friend Kortright for safekeeping. Kortright and his partner, Hugh Mulligan, found a place for Hamilton to stay while in New York. Mulligan's brother, Hercules, was a tailor who lived above his shop on Water Street. Hamilton would stay there.

Knox had given Hamilton letters of introduction to two leading Presbyterian ministers in New York City. Their names were John Rodgers and John Mason. After meeting Hamilton, Rodgers and Mason realized he had never been to school. They agreed he would need some formal schooling before he could enter college. They decided he should attend the Presbyterian Academy at Elizabethtown, New Jersey.

Becoming a College Student

Hamilton journeyed to Elizabethtown and enrolled in the academy. It was located in a two-story building and run by Francis Barber. In class, Hamilton studied Latin, Greek, French, history, literature, philosophy, and mathematics. In the evenings, he often stayed up late, studying by candlelight. He was determined to get to college as quickly as possible. In less than a year, he knew enough to qualify for entrance into college.

Knox had wanted to send Hamilton to the College of New Jersey in Princeton (present-day Princeton University). Hercules Mulligan traveled with Hamilton to Princeton to meet the college president, Dr. John Witherspoon. During his interview, Hamilton explained that he wanted to advance quickly through college. He wanted to take his exams as fast as he learned his subjects. He did not want to follow the regular class programs. "Dr. Witherspoon," recalled Hercules Mulligan, "listened with great attention to so unusual a proposition from so young a person."[1] In the end, the college president decided he could not give one student such special consideration. Hamilton and Mulligan returned to New York City. At an interview at King's College (present-day Columbia University), Hamilton made the same proposal. He was excited to be accepted there. He entered King's College as a sophomore in the fall of 1773.

In 1773, King's College was located in a three-story building on lower Broadway. Today, Columbia University is located in the Harlem section of New York City. Hamilton studied hard at college. He did well in his language classes. For a time, he took an interest in biology. He thought he might become a medical doctor.

"No Taxation Without Representation!"

The spirit of revolution was beginning to take hold in New York when Alexander Hamilton first arrived there. In the 1600s and 1700s, Great Britain established thirteen colonies along the Atlantic coast of North America. Great Britain's royal government appointed governors and other officials to rule these colonies. The colonists elected their own governing assemblies. But new laws sometimes were sent from Great Britain that the colonists were required to obey.

In 1765, American colonists protested a new British law called the Stamp Act. The Stamp Act taxed almost everything written or printed on paper. Pamphlets, newspapers, advertisements, deeds, and even playing cards were taxed. The British government had passed the Stamp Act to help pay the cost of the French and Indian War. That war, which occurred from 1754 to 1763, had been fought to protect the colonists. Therefore, the British government believed the colonists should pay a large part of its cost.

Throughout the thirteen colonies, people were outraged by the Stamp Act. They did not want to pay the tax. The colonists were most upset because they had never been allowed a voice or vote in the British government. They had no elected representatives. To protest the tax, many colonists chanted the slogan "No Taxation Without Representation!"

The British government did away with the Stamp Act in 1766. The following year, however, it passed new laws called the Townshend Acts. These laws taxed such items imported by the colonists as glass, paint, lead, cloth, wine, and tea. In Massachusetts, Samuel Adams had organized a group of angry protesters called the Sons of Liberty. On December 16, 1773, dozens of protesters disguised themselves as American Indians. That night, they boarded three cargo ships anchored in Boston Harbor. They dumped 342 chests of tea into the water. This protest became known as the Boston Tea Party. In time, protesters who demanded an open revolt against British rule became known as revolutionaries.

The British government responded harshly to the Boston Tea Party. The next year, regiments of British soldiers landed in Boston. Massachusetts became occupied territory under military law. All of the thirteen colonies now clearly understood the result of defying unfair British laws.

Angry Boston citizens show what they think of a British tax collector. They have tarred and feathered the man and are forcing him to drink tea. The British tax on tea helped spark the Revolutionary War.

"A Friend to America"

After the Boston Tea Party, Hamilton took a serious interest in the colonists' protests. He found he agreed with many of the protesters. His friend Hercules Mulligan was a revolutionary. Elias Boudinot, William Livingston, and other gentlemen he had met in Elizabethtown, New Jersey, also demanded revolutionary change. There were Americans who agreed with British policies. They were called loyalists. But by December 1774, Hamilton had decided to join the revolutionaries. He would rebel against the British government.

That month, he published a pamphlet he had written. It was a reply to the loyalist pamphlets of New Yorker Samuel Seabury. Hamilton's essay attacked British taxes. He signed it "A Friend to America." In it, he jokingly warned colonists that the British might in time "find means to tax you . . . for every kiss your daughters received from their sweethearts, and, God knows, that would soon ruin you."[2]

Hamilton published a second pamphlet in February 1775. In it, he insisted every man had "an inviolable right to personal liberty and personal safety."[3] No one knew who the writer of these two revolutionary pamphlets was. There was a rumor at King's College that it was Hamilton. But one of his professors, Dr. Myles Cooper, thought it was "absurd to imagine that so young a man" as his own student "could have written them."[4]

On April 19, 1775, British soldiers clashed with local militiamen in Lexington, Massachusetts. When the gun smoke cleared, eighteen rebel colonists lay dead or wounded on the village green. The British soldiers marched on to the town of Concord, searching for rebel arms. During their return to Boston, swarms of fast-arriving colonial "minutemen" attacked them along the road. The Battles of Lexington and Concord marked the bloody beginning of the Revolutionary War.

Volunteer Soldier

As the war began, Hamilton decided that he must take part. He joined a volunteer militia company with some of his college friends. Every morning, with his fellow college volunteers, Hamilton went into St. George's Churchyard, near the college. Together they practiced marching with muskets on their shoulders. On June 25, 1775, Hamilton saw General George Washington for the first time. Washington had been chosen by the Continental Congress as commander in chief of the Continental army. He was riding

A Noble Act

On a night in May 1775, a mob of rebels broke down the King's College gate. They surged into the college yard. They planned to tar and feather Dr. Myles Cooper, if they could find him. Cooper was an outspoken loyalist, a supporter of Great Britain. Out of respect for his professor, Hamilton climbed the building steps as the mob approached. In an emotional speech, he told the mob it must not bring "disgrace on the cause of liberty."[5] While the people listened, Dr. Cooper had just enough time to escape out of a back door.

through New York City on his way to join the troops in Cambridge, Massachusetts.

Fort George was the fort that protected New York Harbor. It was located on the southern tip of Manhattan Island. That summer of 1775, the revolutionary government of New York ordered the cannons in Fort George removed. They were to be brought out of the reach of the British. On the night of August 23, Hamilton joined volunteer militiamen in removing the cannons. A British warship in the harbor, the *Asia*, tried to stop them. It fired its cannons into the city streets. Hercules Mulligan was among the Americans there that night at Fort George. He remembered that "[Hamilton] gave me his musket to hold."[6] Hamilton

Located at the southern tip of Manhattan Island, Fort George guarded New York Harbor. On the night of August 23, 1775, Hamilton helped remove cannons from the fort.

wanted to join in pulling one of the cannon ropes. All twenty-one of the fort's cannons were successfully dragged away.

When the work was finished, Hamilton asked Mulligan to return his musket. Mulligan had to admit he had dropped it when the *Asia* started firing its cannons. Fearlessly, Hamilton returned to the water-front. The *Asia* and other British warships were still sending cannonballs into the streets. But Hamilton calmly found his musket, declared Mulligan, "as if the warship were not there."[7]

Captain of Artillery

In January 1776, the revolutionary government of New York ordered that an artillery company be raised for defense of the colony. Hamilton sent a letter, asking that he be chosen leader of the artillery company. On March 14, 1776, his request was granted. Twenty-one-year-old Hamilton advanced from the rank of private to captain. He had become New York's highest ranking artillery officer. Immediately, he set about enlisting artillery volunteers. He provided them with uniforms and made them learn how to fire cannons. In time, his company numbered sixty-eight officers and enlisted men.

Alexander Hamilton as he looked in his uniform as a captain of artillery.

In Massachusetts, General Washington had forced the British army to leave Boston in March 1776.

He guessed British general Sir William Howe would sail his army to New York City. Washington immediately marched his Continental troops south. In April, Hamilton's New Yorkers joined Washington's Continental army. Hamilton's artillerymen now served under Colonel Henry Knox. Knox gave Hamilton command of the cannons located in Fort George.

Through the first days of July, the American troops prepared defenses on Manhattan and on neighboring Long Island. On July 6, 1776, a messenger brought exciting news into New York City. Hamilton learned the Declaration of Independence had been adopted by the members of the Continental Congress in Philadelphia on July 4. The thirteen colonies had become the United States. They had declared their freedom from British rule.

A huge fleet of British warships and troopships sailed into New York Bay on July 12, 1776. Now it was certain British general Howe hoped to capture New York City. One British scout ship sailed up the Hudson River past Fort George. One of Hamilton's old cannons exploded when it fired upon the ship. Six of his men were killed, and five wounded.

Escape From Manhattan

On August 21, 1776, General Howe began landing his army on Long Island. It included twenty-four thousand British and eight thousand Hessian troops. The Hessians were German soldiers who fought for British king George III in exchange for money. To meet the invasion, Washington had no more than twenty-one thousand Continental soldiers.

On August 27, Washington fought the enemy at the Battle of Brooklyn Heights on Long Island. Nearly surrounded, the Americans were forced to make a hurried retreat. In boats, they ferried across the East River and landed on Manhattan. Within days, the advancing British landed on the east side of Manhattan, too.

During this time, Hamilton and his artillerymen had remained at Fort George. These troops and other American soldiers in New York City realized their danger. They must escape the city or be captured. On a rainy September day, Hamilton marched his artillerymen eight miles north. They escaped to Harlem Heights in the northern part of Manhattan. The heaviest cannons of the fort had to be left behind. Hamilton's soldiers could only bring along two field pieces, cannons of lighter weight on wheeled carriages.

In Full Retreat

By November 1776, Washington's army was retreating across New Jersey. They were closely chased by Howe's British troops. As the days passed, Captain Hamilton's artillery company grew ragged and discouraged.

On November 30, the Continental army crossed the Raritan River into New Brunswick, New Jersey. British troops soon appeared on the opposite side of the river. For a time, Captain Hamilton fired his two cannons across the water. The British were unable to cross the river. It allowed the American troops more time to escape. George Washington Parke Custis, Washington's step-grandson, later remarked that

Washington was impressed "by the brilliant courage and admirable skill" shown by Hamilton.[8]

Eventually, Hamilton and his artillerymen rejoined the Continental army's retreat. One officer recalled seeing Hamilton on the march. He "noticed a youth . . . small, slender, almost delicate in frame, marching . . . with a cocked hat pulled down over his eyes, apparently lost in thought, with his hand resting on a cannon, and every now and then patting it, as if it were a favorite horse or a pet plaything."[9]

The Battle of Trenton

Washington's army retreated all the way across the Delaware River and into Pennsylvania. Hamilton's company camped with most of the army in Bucks County. By this time, the artillery company had dropped to less than thirty men.

Surprisingly, the British troops did not follow their enemy into Pennsylvania. Winter was fast approaching. Howe was content to return to the warm quarters of New York City with most of his army. To control New Jersey, he left behind several strong Hessian outposts stretched across the state.

Colonel Johann Rall commanded the Hessian outpost at Trenton, New Jersey. Rall and his Hessians were not worried about the American troops across the Delaware River. Instead, in December, they relaxed and prepared for the Christmas holiday. It was then that Washington developed a daring plan of attack.

On Christmas night 1776, Hamilton's ragged artillerymen joined a secret march to McKonkey's Ferry on the Delaware River. Heavy snow fell and the river was thick with floating ice. After midnight, Hamilton's company climbed aboard the boats ferrying the army across to New Jersey. When they landed, they joined the army on a difficult march nine miles south to Trenton. By dawn, they entered the town and caught the Hessians completely by surprise.

Too late, Colonel Rall called his sleepy troops out of their quarters. Captain Hamilton had placed his two cannons on the high ground at the end of King Street. American artillery captain Thomas Forrest set other cannons at the end of Queen Street, which ran parallel. When the Hessians charged up those streets,

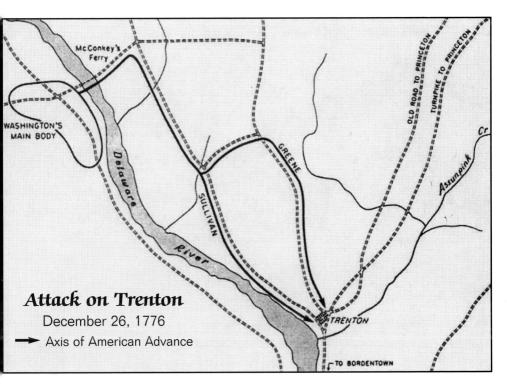

Map of the attack on Trenton

James Monroe at Trenton

Lieutenant James Monroe was an eighteen-year-old Virginian. At the Battle of Trenton, he was one of the few American soldiers wounded. He fell with a bullet in his shoulder. Monroe survived and continued a long career as an American patriot. In 1816, he was elected fifth president of the United States.

they were torn to pieces by cannon fire. About nine hundred Hessian soldiers were captured in the battle. The Americans suffered only two men killed and four wounded.[10] The surprise attack at Trenton had been a stunning victory for the American troops.

Soon after, Washington stung the enemy again. With a quick night march, the Americans attacked the British garrison at Princeton, New Jersey. It is uncertain if Hamilton took part in the Battle of Princeton on January 2, 1777. But it is known there was some American artillery in action.

After that fight, Washington camped most of the Continental army at Morristown, New Jersey, for the winter. Hamilton's artillery company, however, remained in camp on the Pennsylvania side of the Delaware River, in Bucks County.

Lieutenant Colonel Hamilton

GENERAL WASHINGTON needed all the help he could get at his headquarters. "The weight of the whole war," staff officer Tench Tilghman explained, "may be said to lay upon his shoulders."[1] Money and supplies were needed to pay the Continental soldiers and keep them equipped. They suffered greatly from a lack of food, shelter, and medicine. Washington was constantly writing to the Continental Congress asking for help. At the same time, as commander in chief, he was planning the war throughout the thirteen states. Washington spent hours writing orders to his generals. "My time is so taken up at my desk," he once remarked, "that I am obliged to neglect many other essential parts of my duty; it is absolutely necessary . . . for me to have persons that can think for me, as well as execute orders."[2]

Washington had heard good reports of Captain Hamilton from General Henry Knox and General Nathaniel Greene. He learned that Hamilton was educated, a skilled writer, and a brave and loyal soldier. In February 1777, Washington invited twenty-two-year-old Hamilton to join his headquarters staff. He would be promoted to the rank of lieutenant colonel. Hamilton accepted the position.

Staff Duties

Within months of his arrival at headquarters, Hamilton had won General Washington's respect. The general grew to depend upon him greatly. "Details of every kind, political and military," one officer

Lieutenant Colonel Hamilton made himself valuable as a staff officer at General Washington's headquarters.

remembered, were entrusted to Hamilton.[3] Sometimes British soldiers were captured or deserters came into camp. Hamilton questioned them for military information. He was also constantly at work as a secretary. He wrote military letters and prepared army reports.

One long report Hamilton prepared suggested a reorganization of the army to make it easier to command. He penned letters to the presidents of the Continental Congress and to important generals with requests and instructions. Soon

French Adventurers

Hamilton's ability to speak French was a welcome skill at army headquarters. There were a number of soldiers from France in camp. They had come to America to join the fight. Some believed in American liberty. Others were in search of fame and fortune. Many of them expected to be given high ranks in the army. Hamilton spent long hours at headquarters speaking with them. He tried to find French soldiers positions in the army that they would accept. But he complained that Congress had promised to make a general out of "every adventurer that came."[4]

after Hamilton joined the staff, a committee of the New York legislature asked him to send regular letters. They wanted news from army headquarters. Hamilton gladly gave the legislature whatever helpful information he could. It was clear Washington grew to rely on Hamilton. Whenever a messenger brought important mail to headquarters, Washington would tell his personal slave servant Billy, "Call Colonel Hamilton."[5] Together, Washington and Hamilton would write responses.

"The Family"

Hamilton became good friends with the other staff officers at headquarters. They were all young men, such as Robert Harrison, Tench Tilghman, and John Laurens. They called themselves "the family," because of their close relationship with General Washington.[6] They lived and worked together, wherever

Washington made his headquarters. The army was often on the move. At one point in the summer of 1777, headquarters was a single room in a New Jersey log cabin. Washington slept on the only bed, while his staff, including Hamilton, slept on the floor.

In time, Hamilton's fellow staff officers came to respect him as a brave soldier and an honest friend. They called him "Ham" or "Hammy."[7] Harrison gave Hamilton another nickname that stuck. He called him "The Little Lion."[8]

The Battle of Brandywine

In the summer of 1777, the twenty-year-old Marquis de Lafayette joined Washington's army. Lafayette was a French nobleman who deeply believed in the American cause. He moved into Washington's head-quarters. Lafayette and Hamilton soon became close friends.

In July, American spies brought Washington news that in New York City British soldiers were boarding ships. It seemed an invasion fleet was being prepared. Hamilton thought he knew where they would attack. "The enemy will have Philadelphia," he guessed, "if they dare make a bold push for it, unless we fight them . . ."[9]

The British did indeed land in Pennsylvania south of Philadelphia. On September 11, 1777, the Continental army attacked the enemy at Brandywine Creek. When Washington rode into battle, Hamilton, Lafayette, and other staff members rode with him. In the thick of the fight, Lafayette was wounded in the leg. The outnumbered American army suffered a defeat

The French Marquis de Lafayette, pictured here, arrived at Washington's headquarters in the summer of 1777. He bravely volunteered to help fight for America's independence. Lafayette and Hamilton became good friends.

at Brandywine and retreated. General Howe's British troops continued their advance on Philadelphia.

As the British marched ahead, Hamilton was ordered with several cavalrymen to destroy flour stored in mills along the Schuylkill River. At all costs, they were not to let the flour be captured by the enemy. The Americans succeeded in destroying the flour. But as they finished, a large force of British cavalrymen galloped onto the scene. Hamilton and four other soldiers jumped into a boat, as the British opened fire. A soldier beside Hamilton fell dead and another was wounded. But the boat escaped down the river. Downstream, Hamilton sent a hurried note to John Hancock, president of the Continental Congress. "If Congress have not yet left Philadelphia, they ought to do it immediately without fail . . ."[10] He realized the British would soon be marching into the city. Congress took his advice. Its members fled for safety to Lancaster, Pennsylvania.

Germantown and Saratoga

British soldiers entered Philadelphia on September 27, 1777. However, General Howe stationed most of his troops outside the city near the village of German-town. On October 3, General Washington attacked the British again. Confused by a heavy fog, the Americans charged in all directions and even fired on each other by mistake. In panic, they fled the Germantown bat-tlefield. There was little Washington and his staff could do but join in the retreat.

Two weeks after Washington's defeat, Americans finally heard good news. At Saratoga, New York,

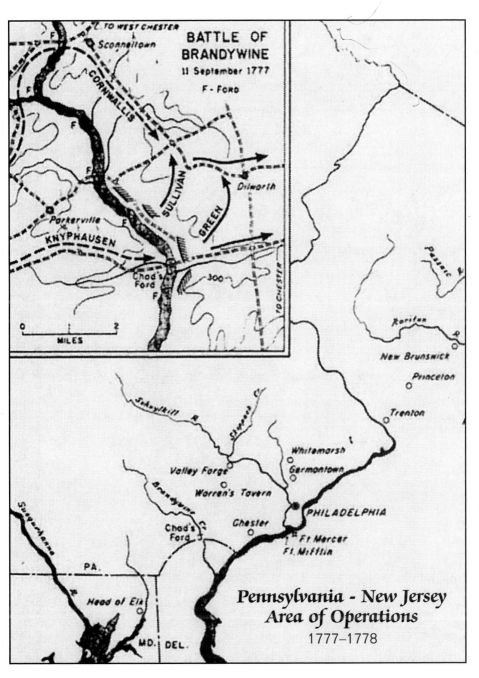

Map of the Battle of Brandywine

General Horatio Gates had won a thrilling victory on October 17. British general John Burgoyne had surrendered his entire army of six thousand troops. The stunning American success at Saratoga marked a turning point in the Revolutionary War. In response to this victory, France recognized American independence. France became an ally of the United States. In time, French warships and army regiments would come to the aid of America.

Just then, however, Washington greatly needed more troops in Pennsylvania. At the end of October, Washington chose Hamilton to ride north and get troops from Gates. Hamilton rode horseback 250 miles to Albany, New York, and met with General Gates. With difficulty, he got Gates to promise to send soldiers south to General Washington. Few soldiers actually ever marched south, however. Gates and New York general Israel Putnam did not want to part with them.

Hamilton's efforts to carry out his orders took their toll. In the cold weather, he fell ill with a fever. For a time, it was thought he would die. In December, New York governor George Clinton sent Dr. John Jones to Hamilton's bedside in Peekskill, New York. Hamilton was fed cooked chicken and given "shrub" to drink as a cure for his illness. Shrub was a drink made of rum and orange juice. On December 19, Colonel Hugh Hughes was finally able to write to General Gates, "Colonel Hamilton, who has been very ill . . . at Peekskill, is out of danger."[11] When he grew well enough, Hamilton rode south to rejoin Washington's army. It was January 20, 1778, when he entered Washington's winter camp at Valley Forge, Pennsylvania.

From Valley Forge to Yorktown

AT VALLEY FORGE, Pennsylvania, Washington's troops had built a city of log cabins on the frozen hills. It was a bitterly cold winter, and the little army lacked warm clothes and food. Huddled close to their fires, the soldiers coughed from the smoke. Hamilton wrote to New York governor George Clinton that unless Washington got help soon "I know not how we shall keep the army together or make another campaign."[1]

General Von Steuben

That winter, a veteran Prussian officer arrived in camp and offered his services. General Washington made Baron Friedrich von Steuben a major general and the Continental army's inspector general. Von Steuben took up the duty of training the troops at

Washington's army survived the freezing cold with thin clothes, poor shelters, and little food during the difficult winter at Valley Forge, Pennsylvania.

Valley Forge. Von Steuben could not speak English, but he spoke French. Hamilton and Colonel John Laurens both spoke French. They were assigned to assist von Steuben. They translated the Baron's orders into English, so he could be understood. Von Steuben taught the troops the proper way to march. He showed them how to load and fire their muskets with speed and skill. The ragged soldiers began to regain confidence.

The Battle of Monmouth

The Continental army survived its hard winter at Valley Forge. As the weather warmed, the troops were ready to fight again. In June 1778, Sir Henry Clinton took command of the British army. Clinton decided to quit Philadelphia. He would march his twelve thousand British soldiers across New Jersey and back to New York City. On June 18, the British troops crossed the Delaware River and began its march. General Washington decided he must follow the enemy with the eleven thousand soldiers of his own Continental army.

Washington had made the Marquis de Lafayette a major general in command of an American army

> *I am sick, discontented, and out of humor. Poor food. Hard lodging. Cold weather. . . . Nasty clothes. Nasty cookery. Vomit half my time. Smoked out of my senses. The Devil's in it. I can't endure it. Why are we sent here to starve and freeze? What sweet [happiness] have I left at home, a charming wife, pretty children, good beds, good food, good cookery. . . . Here all is confusion, smoke and cold, hunger and filthiness. A [curse] on my bad luck.[2]*

Army doctor Albigence Waldo kept a diary while at Valley Forge. In it, he described some of the hardships the American troops suffered.

division. On the march, Hamilton was assigned to assist General Lafayette and keep Washington informed of his progress. On June 26, Hamilton reported that the British had reached Monmouth Court House (present-day Freehold, New Jersey). Washington decided to attack. He gave General Charles Lee command of the troops that would lead the effort.

At dawn, on June 28, 1778, the Battle of Monmouth began. It was a terribly hot day. The temperature rose above 96 degrees Fahrenheit. "The weather was almost too hot to live in," a soldier recalled. The fields, he remembered, felt "like the mouth of a heated oven."[3]

In the end, it was up to Washington to rally the troops personally. "The General rode forward," Hamilton recalled, "and found the troops retiring in the greatest disorder and the enemy pressing upon their rear. . . . He instantly took measures for checking the enemy's advance . . ."[4] Hamilton also showed courage during the fight. During the battle, his horse was wounded and fell. Hamilton was thrown roughly to the ground.

Darkness ended the battle in a draw. Washington planned to continue the fight the next morning. But General Clinton marched his British troops away in the night on to New York City. The Battle of Monmouth had shown that the Americans could match Great Britain's best soldiers.

Romance at Morristown

Day after day, the Americans hoped for the arrival of French troops to join the fight against the British.

While waiting, Washington kept his ragged army together as well as he could. He made Morristown, New Jersey, his winter headquarters again in 1779–1780. It was a cold winter. Snow fell in drifts six feet deep in places. In November 1779, a young woman, Elizabeth "Betsy" Schuyler, arrived near Morristown. She had come on a visit to her uncle, Dr. John Cochran. Tench Tilghman described Betsy as "a brunette with the most good-natured, lively dark eyes that I ever saw."[5] She belonged to one of the richest families in New York. Her father, General Philip Schuyler, owned large estates that covered thousands of acres of land. He was also a member of Congress.

After meeting Elizabeth Schuyler, Hamilton fell in love. On March 8, 1780, he wrote to one of her sisters, Margarita, "Your sister has found out the secret of interesting me in everything that concerns her."[6]

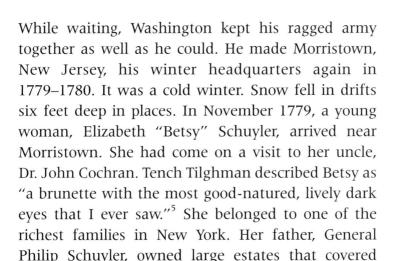

In the winter of 1779, Elizabeth Schuyler visited the American military camp at Morristown, New Jersey. Alexander Hamilton soon fell in love with her.

That month, General Schuyler arrived at Washington's headquarters on military business. Already Betsy Schuyler had promised to marry Hamilton. Now Hamilton respectfully spoke to General Schuyler to ask for his permission. General Schuyler welcomed the engagement. He recognized Hamilton's many talents as an officer and as a brilliant young man. Schuyler would say later, that in making Betsy his wife, "Alexander Hamilton did honor to the Schuyler family."[7]

> "*I* love you more and more every hour. The sweet softness and delicacy of your mind and manners . . . the real goodness of your heart—its tenderness to me—the beauties of your face and person—your unpretending good sense . . . all these . . . place you . . . above all the rest of your sex. . . . *I* . . . love you too much. You engross my thoughts too entirely to allow me to think anything else. You not only employ my mind all day, but you intrude on my sleep. *I* meet you in every dream . . ."[8]

Betsy Schuyler returned home to her family estate in the summer of 1780. Hamilton wrote her this letter.

Benedict Arnold

General Benedict Arnold was one of General Washington's bravest and most trusted officers. In August 1779, Washington assigned Arnold command of the American fort at West Point, New York. The fort guarded the length of the Hudson River.

But Arnold was in need of money and was bitter he had not been given a higher command. He made secret arrangements to surrender the fort to the British. Arnold gave British spy Major John Andre the information needed to carry out the plan. Before Andre could reach British lines, however, American soldiers captured him. They found Arnold's plans hidden in his boot. News of Andre's capture sent Arnold fleeing down the Hudson River by boat on September 15, 1780.

That very day, General Washington and staff officers arrived at West Point to inspect the fort. General Arnold was not there to greet them. Washington soon learned why. A letter arrived from American colonel John Jameson. It described the capture of Major Andre. Hamilton and Lafayette saw tears in Washington's eyes after he read the letter. "Arnold has betrayed us!" the general exclaimed, ". . . Whom can we trust now?"[9]

Washington ordered Hamilton and staff officer James McHenry to gallop south a dozen miles to King's Ferry. They were to try to prevent Arnold's escape. But they arrived too late. Already Arnold had sailed past. Hamilton wrote a hurried note to General Nathaniel Greene: "There has just been unfolded at this place a scene of the blackest treason. Arnold has fled to the enemy."[10]

A Happy Wedding

"A few weeks more and you are mine," Hamilton wrote to his fiancée Betsy Schuyler in October 1780.[11] At the end of November, Hamilton took leave from the army. He rode north for his wedding. He arrived

The Hanging of a Spy

British major John Andre was kept under guard in a village tavern at Tappan, New York, near Washington's headquarters. A military court soon condemned him to death as a spy. Hamilton was a witness at his hanging on October 2, 1780. Andre was asked if he had any last words. He answered, "Nothing, but to request you will witness to the world, that I die like a brave man."[12]

at the Schuyler mansion, which overlooked the Hudson River near Albany, New York.

On December 14, 1780, twenty-six-year-old Alexander Hamilton and twenty-three-year-old Betsy Schuyler were married in the Schuyler's drawing room. General Schuyler told Hamilton, "You cannot my dear Sir be more happy in the connection you have made with my family than I am."[13] Elizabeth's sister, Angelica, later wrote to her, "Ah! Bess! You were a lucky girl to get so clever and so good a companion."[14]

In early January 1781, Hamilton returned to army headquarters now located at New Windsor, New York. Betsy soon joined her husband there. Washington and his wife Martha warmly welcomed them.

A Fateful Argument

For some time, Hamilton had tried to obtain army duty outside of headquarters. "I have," he complained, "no passion for scribbling."[15] He longed for a battlefield command. He told friends he wanted to hear again "the charming sound of bullets."[16]

Washington already had refused to let him go twice. Hamilton's skills as a staff officer were too valuable at headquarters.

On February 16, 1781, Hamilton was hurrying down the stairs at the New Windsor headquarters with some papers. He passed Washington going up the stairs. Washington ordered Hamilton to join him in his room as soon as he had delivered the papers.

Downstairs, Hamilton quickly gave the papers to Tench Tilghman. As he was returning, General Lafayette stopped him and began to chat. Hamilton politely listened a minute and then continued upstairs. As he climbed the steps, Hamilton saw Washington staring down at him.

After his wedding to Elizabeth Schuyler, Hamilton returned to duty at Washington's headquarters in New Windsor, New York. General Washington and his wife Martha welcomed Hamilton and his new bride by throwing a wedding party.

"Colonel Hamilton," Washington coldly said, "you have kept me waiting at the head of the stairs these ten minutes. I must tell you, sir, you treat me with disrespect!"

Hamilton had not expected to be greeted in this way. He responded, "I am not conscious of it, sir, but, since you have thought it necessary to tell me so, we part." He had decided to use this small argument as an excuse to leave headquarters staff duty at last.[17]

Hamilton had worked hard. He felt his contributions to the war effort were not fully appreciated. He offered to stay at headquarters only until a replacement officer could be found. Washington later kindly suggested they forget their argument. But Hamilton believed he had earned the right to battlefield duty.

The March to Virginia

It was not until July 31, 1781, that Washington found a new position for Hamilton. Hamilton received command of a battalion of four New York infantry companies. The battalion was part of the division commanded by Lafayette. This was exactly the kind of position Hamilton had wanted.

That summer, Washington saw a sudden chance for victory. A French army of 7,800 men commanded by the Comte de Rochambeau had joined the 9,000 American troops in Washington's New York camp. A large French fleet was also soon expected to reach Chesapeake Bay.

For some time, British general Lord Charles Cornwallis had been marching an army through the Carolinas and into Virginia. At the end of the summer, he had reached the Virginia coast. His troops were now encamped at the village of Yorktown. Washington realized he had an excellent chance to defeat Cornwallis. He immediately started his soldiers on a hurried march south. "A part of the army, my dear girl, is going to Virginia," Hamilton excitedly wrote to his wife.[18] As the march began, two companies of Connecticut troops were added to Hamilton's battalion. With hard marching, the American and French troops reached Yorktown on September 28.

Siege Warfare

Washington decided to lay siege to Yorktown. He would not order his infantry to charge ahead and

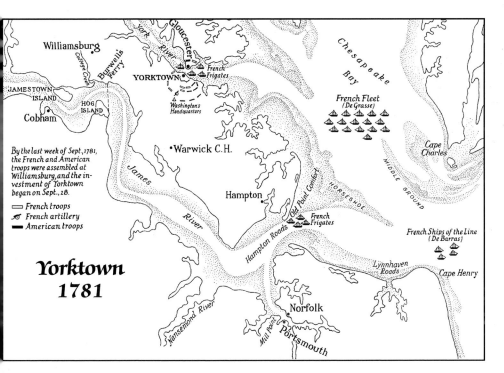

Map of the siege of Yorktown

attack the enemy position. Instead, he would use his cannons to bombard the town. The bombardment of Yorktown began on October 9, 1781. To bring the cannons into better range, soldiers armed with shovels dug a series of trenches. Each day, the American and French cannons were dragged closer and closer to Yorktown.

In time, Washington realized two small British forts, called Redoubts #9 and #10, would have to be captured. The redoubts prevented the allied trenches from advancing any closer to Yorktown. It was decided French soldiers would attack Redoubt #9. Hamilton persuaded Washington to give him command of the attack on Redoubt #10. Hamilton left the general's tent with a smile. Major Nicholas Fish was second-in-command of Hamilton's battalion. He remembered that Hamilton ran up to him shouting, "We have it! We have it!"[19]

The Night Attack

The surprise attack was planned for the night of October 14, 1781. The firing of cannons signaled the moment to start forward. The French hurried ahead through the darkness toward Redoubt #9. On the right, Hamilton's four hundred men jumped up from the nearest trenches. They rushed toward Redoubt #10.

Hamilton had told his troops not to load their muskets. He was afraid an accidental gunshot would alert the enemy. Instead, he told them to rely on their sharply pointed bayonets to kill the British defenders. As they rushed toward the redoubt, the British began shooting at them. Sharpened logs, called "abatis," surrounded the redoubts as added protection. They were like giant spears pointed outward. Some American soldiers carried axes to chop a path, while the other troops waited.

Unwilling to wait, Hamilton squeezed through the abatis and began climbing the high dirt redoubt wall. Other soldiers followed. He and his brave men soon overwhelmed the enemy. Redoubt #10 was quickly captured. About sixty British and Hessian soldiers surrendered. Hamilton later declared, "From the firing of the first shot by the enemy to their surrender was less than ten minutes."[20] He was proud of his success in battle. To his wife, he later wrote, "I commanded an attack upon one of the enemy's redoubts; we carried it in an instant, and with little loss . . ."[21] In fact, nine American soldiers had been killed and thirty-one wounded in the attack.

The capture of the two enemy redoubts greatly hurt the British. Washington was able to bring his cannons

This is a painting of the surrender of the British army at Yorktown, Virginia, October 19, 1781.

within close range of Yorktown. Soon cannonballs pounded every part of the town. On October 17, Cornwallis admitted his defeat. Hamilton attended the surrender of the British army two days later. But afterwards, he immediately hurried north to Albany. Betsy Hamilton was pregnant with their first child. Hamilton wanted to be at home when the baby was born. On January 22, 1782, their child was born: a son named Philip, in honor of his grandfather.

Lawyer and Congressman

THE BATTLE OF YORKTOWN ended Hamilton's service in the Continental army. He remained in Albany. "I sigh for nothing but the company of my wife and baby," he declared.[1] In November 1782, he happily wrote to Lafayette, "I have been employed for the last ten months in rocking the cradle."[2]

Upon leaving the army, Hamilton decided to begin "studies relative to my future career in life."[3] New York lawyer James Duane wrote to him, "I am much pleased to find that you have set yourself seriously to the study of the law."[4] Hamilton began his law studies in January 1782. Duane helped by loaning him law books. That April, one of Hamilton's college friends, Robert Troup, had become a lawyer. Troup moved in with the Hamiltons and assisted Hamilton in his reading. Troup later recalled that Hamilton's habit was to walk back and forth while studying a book. He joked that Hamilton had walked long enough to have traversed the continent while studying law.[5] In six months' time, Hamilton was fully qualified and accepted by the state supreme court as a New York lawyer.

Tax Collector

Hamilton was still studying his law books on May 2, 1782, when he received a letter offering him

Robert Morris was superintendent of finance for the Continental government. He asked Hamilton to become the government's tax collector in the state of New York.

a job. Robert Morris was the chief treasury official of the Continental government. Morris invited Hamilton to become the New York receiver of Continental taxes. Unless Congress obtained money, independence could still fail. No peace treaty between the United States and Great Britain had yet been signed. The Continental army was still in the field and needed to be maintained. Hamilton was unwilling to interrupt his law studies, but he finally accepted. In July, he journeyed to

Poughkeepsie, New York, for the special meeting of the state legislature.

Congress had asked the states for $8 million. It had received only $400,000. Robert Morris said that getting money from the states was "like preaching to the dead."[6] Hamilton had little success in collecting money from the New York state legislature. But he made a good impression on the politicians he met. On July 22, 1782, the legislature elected him a delegate to Congress.

New York Congressman

"I am going to throw away a few more months in public life," Hamilton wrote the Marquis de Lafayette, "and then I retire a simple citizen . . . "[7] Hamilton journeyed south to Philadelphia and took his seat in Congress on November 25, 1782. On that day, he resigned his job as a Continental tax collector.

In Congress, Hamilton met James Madison, James Wilson of Pennsylvania, John Rutledge of South Carolina, and other important congressmen. His old friend from New Jersey, Elias Boudinot, was serving as president of Congress. Hamilton went to work with energy. He served on committees, wrote reports, and joined in the debates.

After the Battle of Yorktown, the Revolutionary War and American independence were practically won. During the next two years, there was little fighting. With each passing month, however, American soldiers continued to demand their pay. But Congress had no money to give them.

On June 21, 1783, about three hundred angry enlisted soldiers marched into Philadelphia. They surrounded the Pennsylvania State House (now Independence Hall) where Congress met. They waved their muskets and shouted curses at the congressmen inside the building. Only at the end of the day did they allow the congressmen to leave. The threats of these unpaid soldiers scared the congressmen. They decided to conduct the government in a safer place. Hamilton recommended to Boudinot that Congress meet in Princeton, New Jersey. In Princeton, Hamilton led the effort in Congress to find money to pay the soldiers. They were finally paid.

During his eight-month term in Congress, Hamilton became one of New York's leading politicians. When he left Congress in July 1783, Hamilton declared, "We have now happily concluded the great work of independence, but much remains to be done to reach the fruits of it."[8]

Starting a Law Career

When the Treaty of Paris was signed in September 1783, the Revolutionary War officially ended. Americans had won their independence. For a time, British troops still occupied New York City. But Hamilton stated that as soon as they left he planned to "set down there seriously on the business of making my fortune."[9] On November 25, 1783, the British army finally left New York. Soon after, Hamilton moved with his wife and son to 57 Wall Street in Manhattan. He began his new career as a lawyer.

Law clerk James Kent remembered seeing Hamilton in court. "His manners were gentle, affable, and kind," Kent recalled.[10] Hamilton's skill as a lawyer put him in great demand. He appeared in city courts as well as the state supreme court. Forty-five of Hamilton's early cases were concerned with New York's Trespass Act. The Trespass Act allowed property owners to recover money from loyalists who had used their property during the war. The most famous of Hamilton's Trespass Act cases was *Rutgers* v. *Waddington*.

Elizabeth Rutgers owned a brewery on Maiden Lane in New York City. She had been a patriotic supporter of the Revolutionary War. She had followed the American army, when it retreated from New York City in September 1776. The British army, while occupying the city, gave loyalist merchant Joshua Waddington the right to run Rutgers's brewery. At the end of the war, Elizabeth Rutgers returned home. She immediately took Waddington to court and sued him under the Trespass Act. She demanded rent for the time Waddington had used her brewery. The case was tried on August 7, 1784, in the Mayor's Court. Alexander Hamilton defended Waddington.

In court, Hamilton argued that when the British seized the brewery, it was behaving according to accepted international law. Waddington owed no rent to Rutgers because he had used her property with the permission of the British in wartime. Hamilton claimed New York's Trespass Act conflicted with the Treaty of Paris. State courts, he argued, must obey national laws. Law clerk James Kent

Hamilton (standing, far right) addressed the judges in a court case. Hamilton was respected in New York for his brilliant courtroom arguments. In the 1700s, lawyers and judges wore black robes and white wigs in court.

attended the trial. He recalled that whenever Hamilton spoke he "soared far above all competition . . . The audience listened with admiration to his impassioned eloquence."[11] On August 27, James Duane, who was serving as a judge, gave the court's decision. During the time he ran the brewery with the British army's permission, Waddington did not owe Elizabeth Rutgers rent.

The Annapolis Convention

In 1781, the Continental Congress had established a national government under a set of laws called the

Articles of Confederation. The Articles, however, were nothing more than a weak agreement between the states. The powers to tax, regulate trade between the states, and raise armies remained state powers. While serving in the army and in Congress, Hamilton had often complained about the weakness of the Articles of Confederation.

In 1785, Congress decided changes needed to be made. It asked the states to appoint delegates to meet in Annapolis, Maryland. The delegates would try to design better national trade laws. Hamilton was chosen to be a delegate from New York. He arrived in Annapolis on September 9, 1786.

Altogether, only five states sent delegates to the convention. They were New York, Virginia, Pennsylvania, Delaware, and New Jersey. Very little could be accomplished. Hamilton seized the moment, however, to write a formal request, which other delegates signed. It recommended that Congress call a second convention. Its purpose would be to "to take into consideration the situation of the United States . . . "[12] A new convention could revise the Articles of Confederation and make the national government stronger. In February 1787, Congress agreed that another convention should meet in Philadelphia. It would gather on the second Monday in May. Twelve states agreed to send delegates. Only Rhode Island refused to take part. Hamilton had great hopes that this Philadelphia convention would change the future of America.

A New National Government

HAMILTON SERVED IN the New York legislature from January to April 1787. One important law he got passed established a New York state university. That spring, the legislature selected its delegates to the Constitutional Convention. They chose Robert Yates, John Lansing, Jr., and Alexander Hamilton to represent the state. Yates and Lansing supported the politics of Governor George Clinton. Clinton was against making the national government stronger. Because convention voting would be by states, Hamilton was outnumbered two to one. Still, he traveled south, hoping the national government could be improved.

The Virginia Plan

Hamilton arrived in Philadelphia in May. He rented a room at the popular Indian Queen tavern on

Third Street. He took his convention seat at the Pennsylvania State House for the first time on May 18, 1787.

The convention had begun to meet on May 14. The delegates had immediately elected George Washington to be convention president. Washington sat at a desk at the front of the assembly room. In all, fifty-five delegates would attend the convention. They included such important men as Benjamin Franklin, James Madison, and James Wilson. They met each day, six days a week, from late morning to early evening.

On the morning of May 29, Virginia delegate Edmund Randolph stood and read to the convention a surprising outline. It included fifteen steps for the creation of a new United States government. The outline came to be called the Virginia Plan. The Articles of Confederation were a failure, the outline declared. In its place, the outline called for a national government

The Pennsylvania State House in Philadelphia was the site where delegates to the Constitutional Convention met in the summer of 1787. Today the building is known as Independence Hall.

consisting of three branches. They were the legislative, executive, and judicial branches. The legislative branch (a Senate and House of Representatives) would make laws. The executive branch (the president) would enforce the laws. The judicial branch (the federal court system) would interpret the laws. Each branch could prevent the other two from becoming too powerful. They could hold in check the actions of the others. It would be a system of checks and balances. James Madison had written most of the Virginia Plan, with some help from fellow Virginia delegate George Mason. After listening to Randolph, the convention voted to design a new government based on the Virginia Plan.

Hamilton's Speech

During his first four weeks at the convention, Hamilton sat quietly. He listened to the debates and took notes. Yates and Lansing quit the convention early. They refused to discuss making such great changes in the government. They returned to New York in protest. Hamilton became New York's only remaining delegate. He did not feel he could represent his entire state during convention votes. But he could still speak his mind.

On June 18, an especially hot day, he finally rose from his seat. He gave a five-hour speech that startled all of his listeners. "We must establish a general and national government," he declared, ". . . and unless we do this, no good purpose can be answered."[1] James Madison kept detailed notes of the convention debates. He wrote that Hamilton revealed that "in his private opinion . . . the British government was the best in the world: and . . . he doubted . . . whether anything short of it would do in America."[2]

Hamilton then suggested his own detailed plan of government. It was a plan greatly influenced by the royal British form of government. Hamilton's plan included the election of a president for life, the election of senators for life, and presidential power to appoint state governors, who would also have life terms. The plan of government he proposed, he admitted, "went beyond the ideas of most members."[3] But he believed it would be the best. Three days after Hamilton spoke, delegate William Samuel Johnson said Hamilton had been "praised by everybody," but "supported by none."[4] Having just won independence from Great Britain, few delegates were willing to accept so close a copy of the British government.

On June 18, 1787, Hamilton addressed the Constitutional Convention. He asked for a strong national government that would be in many ways like the royal British government. Although they respected his opinion, most delegates did not like his ideas.

The Three-fifths Decision

Hamilton left the convention on June 29 and returned to New York. "I wish you were back," George Washington wrote to him.[5] He remained away during July and part of August. During that time, delegates debated on how the House of Representatives should be structured and how representatives should be chosen. After much discussion, it was decided the number of representatives would be decided according to state populations. Southerners wanted their slaves to count fully in the population. Northerners were against that idea. In a compromise, the delegates agreed that slaves would be counted as equal to three-fifths of a free white citizen. Hamilton later admitted that without this agreement "no union could possibly have been formed."[6]

Hamilton returned to the convention for the week of August 13–20. He also attended the final two weeks, September 2–17. In September, he wrote in his notes that he would "take any system which promises to save America."[7]

Signing the Constitution

On September 8, 1787, a committee was chosen to prepare the final wording of the Constitution. The five men selected were Gouverneur Morris, William Samuel Johnson, Rufus King, James Madison, and Alexander Hamilton. They were called the Committee of Style and Arrangement. It took them four days to finish their work. Gouverneur Morris did the actual writing.

On September 17, 1787, thirty-eight delegates remained in Philadelphia. Some delegates had been called home by their state governments. Others, like Yates and Lansing, had walked out of the convention when things did not go their way.

The Constitution was read aloud on September 17. Afterwards, Benjamin Franklin rose with a speech in his hand. The old patriot did not have the energy to read it himself. James Wilson did that for him. "Mr. President," Franklin had written, "I confess that there are several parts of this Constitution which I do not at present approve . . . " But he added, "I consent, Sir, to this Constitution, because I expect no better and because I am not sure that it is not the best."[8] Hamilton felt the same way. The Constitution did not include the powers he had recommended. Still, it created a stronger national government. Hamilton knew it would be good for the United States.[9]

The moment arrived at last for the signing of the Constitution. In his eagerness to see it signed, Hamilton stepped to the president's desk. He wrote the names of each of the states on the document, ready to receive the signatures of their delegates. As the only delegate remaining from his state, Alexander Hamilton became the only New York signer of the Constitution.

The Federalist

The signers of the Constitution were amazed at what they had accomplished. George Washington called it "little short of a miracle."[10] Just eight days after receiving the Constitution, Congress recommended that the states call conventions to ratify the document. Ratifying it meant the states would officially accept it.

Some Americans angrily asked who had given these men at Philadelphia the power to design a totally new government. Thirty-year-old Alexander Hamilton believed the public must be persuaded to support the Constitution. In October, he decided to write a series of newspaper essays defending the Constitution. He invited James Madison and John Jay to join him in this important effort. Eighty-five articles were published during the next months. Hamilton wrote fifty-one, Madison twenty-nine, and Jay, who fell ill, five. The articles appeared from October 1787 until April 1788. They were signed "Publius" (Latin for "the Public Man").[11] When a book of the collected essays was published in the spring of 1788, it was titled *The Federalist*.

In his first article, Hamilton addressed the "People of the State of New York."[12] It appeared in the New York *Independent Journal* on October 27, 1787. "The people of this country," Hamilton declared, "[must] decide the important question [whether] societies of men are really [able] or not of establishing good government . . . "[13] In article No. 11, Hamilton exclaimed, "Let the thirteen States, bound together in . . . Union, [agree to build] one great American system . . ."[14] "A nation without a national government is . . . an awful spectacle," he stated in his final essay.[15]

On September 17, 1787, Benjamin Franklin called upon delegates to sign the Constitution. Hamilton agreed with Franklin that the Constitution would make the United States a better country.

The Federalist had a great effect on its readers. Many Americans were persuaded of the importance of ratifying the Constitution. George Washington believed the collected essays would be important forever, because they skillfully "discussed . . . principles of freedom and . . . topics of government, which will be always interesting to mankind . . . "[16]

Secretary of the Treasury

HAMILTON WAS NAMED a delegate to New York's ratification convention. It met in Poughkeepsie in June 1788. With strong arguments, Hamilton spent the next weeks defending the Constitution. At last, on July 26, the convention voted to ratify in a close decision. Hamilton hurried to New York City and immediately presented the news to Congress. New York was the eleventh state to ratify. North Carolina and Rhode Island would both do so by 1790. But already the nation's new constitutional government had begun.

Most Americans wanted George Washington to become the country's first president. Hamilton personally urged the respected general to accept the duty. According to the Constitution, each state chose electors. The electors voted for candidates for president and vice president. They chose Washington to be president and John Adams to be vice president. On April 30, 1789, Hamilton watched Washington's inauguration from the window of his house on Wall Street. On the balcony of Federal Hall across the street, Washington took the oath of office as first president of the United States. A new chapter had begun in United States history.

Choosing a Cabinet

In May 1789, Congress agreed that department secretaries should be appointed by the president. Laws establishing the Department of State and the

The large building on Wall Street in New York City is the Federal Hall where George Washington took oath as first president of the United States in 1789. At the end of the street is Trinity Church where Hamilton regularly attended Sunday services.

Department of War were passed in July and August. The Department of the Treasury was created on September 2. It was decided the yearly salary for the secretary of the treasury would be $3,500. Today, the secretary of the treasury earns $161,200 a year.

For his Cabinet officers, President Washington picked Thomas Jefferson to be secretary of state. He chose Henry Knox to be secretary of war. For attorney general, he selected Edmund Randolph. Washington asked Robert Morris for advice on the best person to name secretary of the treasury. "What are we to do with this heavy debt?" Washington wondered. Morris

President George Washington picked the best people he could to fill his Cabinet. He chose Alexander Hamilton to become the first secretary of the Department of Treasury.

replied, "There is but one man in the United States who can tell you; that is, Alexander Hamilton."[1] On September 11, 1789, Washington nominated Hamilton secretary of the treasury. The Senate voted to accept Hamilton for the office the same day.

Hamilton had the least government experience of any of the Cabinet officers Washington had chosen. Thomas Jefferson had been minister to France. Henry Knox had been a Revolutionary War general. Hamilton's only qualifications were that he had read some books on economics and written some papers on the subject. On September 13, Hamilton entered the Treasury Department on Broadway. He immediately took up his new duties. A visitor to the treasury office found Hamilton seated at a simple pine table covered with a green cloth.

In 1789, the Treasury Department had a staff of only five people. During the next year, it grew to over thirty clerks. It was the largest of the government departments. In addition, Hamilton was in charge of five hundred customs agents. It was the job of the customs agents to collect taxes on ship cargoes arriving in the United States. It was a major source of government income. Hamilton ordered a fleet of fast boats built for his customs agents. When ships docked, the customs agents boarded and examined the cargoes. Customs boats cruised the Atlantic coast to prevent smuggling. Smugglers tried to sneak their cargoes into the country without paying taxes.

"Report on Public Credit"

"Most of the important measures of every Government are connected with the Treasury," Hamilton once declared.[2] Hamilton believed the success of the United States depended on its economic policies. On September 21, 1789, the House of Representatives asked Hamilton to prepare a plan. It wanted his thoughts on how to establish national credit.

Hamilton began designing plans for the economic future of the country. The Revolutionary War had cost a lot of money. The United States owed foreign banks about $50 million. This was a huge amount of money

Advice on Manners

Soon after taking office, President Washington asked Hamilton for advice on presidential manners. Washington needed help in deciding how a president should behave. Hamilton suggested the president make three kinds of regular social appearances. He suggested a weekly "levee," or reception, open to the public. He also suggested Washington sometimes give small family dinners, with several invited guests. Finally, he proposed that Washington give a few grand, formal dinners each year, which congressmen, Cabinet members, and foreign diplomats could attend. Washington carried out all of Hamilton's advice.

for a small nation of 4 million people to pay. Hamilton finally sent his "Report on the Public Credit" to the House of Representatives on January 14, 1790. Most congressmen had expected him to give basic suggestions for handling the public debt. Instead they received a detailed forty thousand-word report.

Hamilton had designed a plan to create a strong, healthy national economy. The United States must pay its debts, Hamilton declared. But he also suggested that it pay the $25 million in war debts owed by the states. Paying these debts, Hamilton insisted, was "the price of liberty."[3] Altogether, Hamilton wanted the government to repay debts of $75 million.

In his report, Hamilton suggested the debts could be paid by existing customs taxes. Additional money could be raised by taxes on alcohol, tea, and coffee.

Paying these debts, state as well as national, he pointed out, was the honorable thing to do. Payment would gain the country economic respect. Foreign banks would gladly loan the United States money in the future, if they trusted they would be paid back.

A Political Bargain

On July 29, 1790, Congress passed the Funding Bill. This law agreed to pay the national debt. The idea of taking on the state debts, however, caused angry debate in Congress. Citizens of states that had large debts thought it was a fine idea. But people in states that had already paid off most of their Revolutionary War debt thought the idea was unfair. Other people resisted the idea because it would increase the power of the national government over the states.

In the summer of 1789, Americans learned a revolution had occurred in France. A radical democratic government was established. Hamilton disliked and distrusted the new French government. Instead, he strongly favored better relations with Great Britain. Thomas Jefferson, however, believed the French Revolution would become another great leap for democracy, like the American Revolution. The two men disagreed on other issues, as well. Hamilton supported the interests of America's businessmen and manufacturers. Jefferson, on the other hand, favored farmers. Jefferson feared the growing power of the national government over the states. Both men worried that the other would destroy the government if he obtained too much influence.

Hamilton's supporters began calling themselves Federalists. They favored a strong federal government. Jefferson's supporters came to be called the Democratic-Republican Party. It was the forerunner of today's Democratic Party. America's political party system grew from the different outlooks of these two men.

Through the winter of 1789, Congress battled over where to locate the permanent national capital. New Englanders preferred New York City. Pennsylvanians desired Philadelphia. Virginians wanted a new capital to be built in the South, on the Maryland side of the Potomac River. Hamilton was willing to let the capital be on the Potomac River. He used his growing political power to strike a bargain. Democratic-Republicans in Congress were to allow state debts to be paid by the national government. In exchange, Hamilton and the Federalists agreed to support the plan for the Potomac capital. On July 24, 1790, a law creating the new District of Columbia was passed. Philadelphia would be the temporary capital until 1800. Then the government would move south to the new Federal District of Columbia. Hamilton got his half of the political bargain, too. A law allowing state debts

This is a portrait of Secretary of State Thomas Jefferson. Hamilton and Jefferson did not agree on many government issues. Their disagreements led to the founding of political parties in the United States.

to be paid by the national government was signed by President Washington on August 4.

A National Bank

In the fall of 1790, Hamilton worked on his next great report to Congress. It called for a national bank, the Bank of the United States. The bank would be allowed to run for twenty years. A bank could raise money for the government by issuing long-term bonds. People who purchased the bonds would be lending the government money. Hamilton's report was sent to the House of Representatives on December 14, 1790.

Congressman James Madison was a Democratic-Republican supporter of Jefferson's politics. He did not want Hamilton to strengthen the powers of the national government even more. "Reviewing the Constitution," Madison declared, "it was not possible to discover in it the power to incorporate a Bank."[4] Pennsylvania senator William Maclay described the Senate debate on the national bank. "Such a scene of confused speeches," he exclaimed, "followed as I have seldom heard before. Every one [pretended] to understand the subject . . . "[5]

Madison lost the debate in Congress. In February 1791, Congress passed a bill creating the Bank of the United States. President Washington was not sure if signing the bill into law would be constitutional. He asked Hamilton to write out his arguments for the bank. Hamilton explained its value in detail. It would help support public credit, he declared. It would be a source of loans. It would also aid the government in collecting taxes and in paying government bills.

Altogether, Hamilton urged, a national bank would help the nation's economy grow. There was nothing in the Constitution about creating a national bank, it was true. But there was nothing in the Constitution to prohibit it. Unless the Constitution said otherwise, Hamilton insisted, the United States had "a right to employ all means" to make the country better.[6]

In the end, President Washington was convinced by Hamilton's arguments. On February 21, 1791, he signed the bill creating the Bank of the United States. In December of that year, the bank's main office opened in Philadelphia. In time, eight more branch offices opened in Boston, New York, Baltimore, Washington, D.C., Norfolk, Charleston, Savannah, and New Orleans.

This is a portrait of Philip Schuyler, Hamilton's father-in-law. Schuyler served as one of New York's first senators in Congress. When he ran for reelection in 1791, however, he was defeated by Aaron Burr.

The Rise of Aaron Burr

Hamilton's father-in-law, Philip Schuyler, had become one of New York's first two senators. But Schuyler had political enemies in the state. In 1791, Schuyler came up for reelection. Governor George Clinton and members of New York's powerful Livingston family looked for a candidate to defeat him. They chose New York attorney general Aaron Burr.

Burr organized Clinton supporters and Federalists and won the election.

The Mint

In its first years, the United States had no money of its own. Americans used the gold, silver, and copper coins of most European nations. Goods and services could be paid for with such coins as English shillings, French pistoles, Spanish doubloons, and Portuguese johannes. Coins in all shapes, sizes, and values were exchanged. Clearly, the United States needed to mint its own money. Thomas Jefferson had earlier suggested a coin system based on hundreds, the decimal system. It included dollar coins, quarters, dimes, and cents. Hamilton agreed this would be a good system. At Hamilton's urging, the Mint Act was passed on April 2, 1792. It established the nation's first mint in Philadelphia.

Hamilton took the defeat of his father-in-law personally. He thought Aaron Burr was not trustworthy. He remarked that "his eyes were opened at last to the true nature of Burr."[7] "As a public man," Hamilton wrote, Burr "is one of the worst sort—a friend to nothing but as it suits his interest and ambition."[8] In time, Hamilton's feelings about Aaron Burr would grow more and more intense.

"Report on Manufactures"

In January 1790, Congress asked that Secretary Hamilton prepare an economic plan. They wanted a plan to make the United States "independent of other nations . . . for military supplies."[9] Hamilton went to work preparing his third important government report. He delivered his "Report on Manufactures" to Congress on December 5, 1791. It described the importance of manufacturing for the future of the country.

At the time, there was little factory production in the United States. Workers were unskilled. Machinery was often crude and worked poorly. Americans had little money to invest in new factories. But Hamilton pointed out, the United States would remain weak if it continued to rely on imported goods. He believed that by promoting manufacturing, skilled foreign workers and businessmen would come to live in America. He also suggested that industry would create a growing demand for America's many natural resources. In addition, manufacturing would put more Americans to work. "Women and children are rendered more useful ... " he pointed out.[10] Hamilton had gone to work at an early age. His mother had opened and run a general store. He thought that American women and children could work if manufacturing grew.[11]

The Society for Establishing Useful Manufactures

While Congress considered Hamilton's report, he made a personal effort to promote American industry. He actively assisted in setting up the Society for Establishing Useful Manufactures. It was the first real attempt to promote industry in the United States. The society planned to develop seven hundred acres beside the Great Falls of the Passaic River in northeastern New Jersey. Hamilton and

Washington had visited the spot during the war. The fifty-foot waterfalls could provide a constant source of power to turn the gears of machines. The society proposed to establish a factory town there.

Hamilton drew up the Society's charter. The charter was granted by the New Jersey legislature on November 22, 1791. In thanks, the Society named its new town Paterson, in honor of New Jersey's governor, William Paterson. In Paterson, the Society planned to establish a mill for the spinning and weaving of cotton into cloth. Hamilton hired Thomas Marshall to run the cotton mill.

Society plans called for future Paterson factories to make paper, shoes, pottery, and many other products. But Hamilton was too hopeful. The Society made mistakes and wasted money. Finally, an expensive cotton mill was built. The production of cotton goods had begun. But management was not yet skilled enough in the United States. Costs to run the mill were too high. In March 1792, the Society for the Establishment of Useful Manufactures went bankrupt. In time,

This is a view of the Great Falls on the Passaic River in New Jersey. It was here that Hamilton chose to establish the mill town of Paterson.

Paterson would fulfill its promise as a thriving industrial city. Cotton mills, silk mills, and even a gun factory run by Samuel Colt would successfully use the power of the Great Falls in the 1800s.

The Reynolds Affair

On a day in July 1791, a twenty-three-year-old woman named Maria Reynolds called at Hamilton's Philadelphia home. She told Hamilton her husband James Reynolds had abandoned her and their young daughter. She begged Hamilton for some money to help her travel home to New York. Hamilton thought her story was odd. But he also admitted he thought she was a "pretty woman in distress."[12] He promised to bring some money to her at her boarding house. That evening, he arrived and was shown the way upstairs to her bedroom. He gave Maria Reynolds thirty dollars. Alone with this pretty woman, however, Hamilton was unable to resist her.

A Healthy Economy

Over time, Hamilton's economic policies met with amazing success. The British earl of Liverpool made a speech in Parliament in 1820. He declared that "America increased in wealth . . . in population, in strength more rapidly than any nation ever before increased in the history of the world."[13] The United States had exported $19 million worth of goods in 1791. In 1801, the figure had jumped to $93 million, an advance of 400 percent.

Hamilton and Maria Reynolds began an affair that continued during the next six months. Usually they met at Hamilton's home when his wife was away. At other times, they met at her boarding house bedroom. In December 1791, Maria Reynolds suddenly told Hamilton that her husband had learned about the affair. James Reynolds soon wrote a letter to Hamilton full of anger and threats. After meeting with Hamilton twice, Reynolds finally said he would keep quiet and forget the affair if Hamilton paid him one thousand dollars.

Hamilton paid this blackmail money. But he also continued visiting Maria Reynolds. James Reynolds made more demands, and Hamilton paid him at least $135 in April, $350 in May, $50 in June, and $200 in August.[14] Only in August 1792 did Hamilton finally end the relationship.

Dark Suspicions

In November 1792, James Reynolds and a criminal partner named Jacob Clingman were arrested. The United States government charged the two men with illegally claiming the pension money of several army veterans. While trying to get out of prison, Clingman asked Pennsylvania congressman Frederick Muhlenberg to visit him. He claimed Reynolds could provide proof that Alexander Hamilton was stealing money from the national treasury. Muhlenberg noted that Clingman "frequently dropped hints to me, that Reynolds had it in his power ... to injure the Secretary of the Treasury."[15]

. . .You have deprived me of every thing thats near and dear to me. . . . Sir you took the advantage of a poor Broken harted woman. instead of being a Friend. you have acted the part of the most Cruelist man in existance. you have mad a whole family miserable. . . . now I am determined to have satisfation. it shant be onely one [f]amily that miserable. for I am Robbed of all happiness in this world. . . . now Sir if I Cant see you at your house call and see me. for there is no person that Knowes any thing as yet." [16]

In his letter to Hamilton, James Reynolds used poor spelling, punctuation, and capitalization. Many Americans could read and write in the 1700s. But they did not always agree on spelling. When Noah Webster published his first dictionary in 1806, he solved many spelling mistakes.

Muhlenberg shared this rumor with two fellow congressmen, Senator James Monroe and Representative Abraham Venable. The three visited Reynolds to learn more. Reynolds showed the three men personal checks made out to him and signed by Hamilton. They were led to believe Reynolds had acted as Hamilton's agent in illegally buying and selling government bonds.

On December 15, 1792, Muhlenberg, Monroe, and Venable entered the treasury office on Chestnut Street in Philadelphia. They told Secretary Hamilton what they had heard. They offered to give him a chance to defend himself. Hamilton asked them to visit him at his home that night.

The three Democratic-Republicans arrived that evening. With Hamilton was his chief treasury assistant, Oliver Wolcott. Deeply embarrassed, Hamilton admitted that he knew Reynolds. He admitted that he had given Reynolds money. But he explained that the payments had nothing to do with treasury business. It was then that he admitted his affair with Reynold's wife. The payments, he proved, had nothing to do with his job as treasury secretary. When they had heard everything, the three congressmen promised to keep silent about Hamilton's sex affair. Hamilton hoped that no more would be said about his shameful secret.

The Whiskey Rebellion

In March 1791, Congress passed a national tax on alcohol. The tax angered many American farmers. Farmers often made whiskey out of their corn crops. Whiskey lasted much longer than corn. Barrels and jugs of whiskey could be brought to market easier. Farmers in western Pennsylvania especially hated the new tax. In September 1791, angry Pennsylvania farmers tarred and feathered the tax collector for Washington and Allegheny counties. In July 1794, an armed mob of farmers set fire to the house of the area's chief tax collector.

Attacks against treasury officials and federal marshals increased. In response, Hamilton called for troops to protect the law. "The very existence of Government demands this course," he exclaimed. "Shall the majority govern or be governed? Shall the nation rule or be ruled? . . . Shall there be government or no government?"[17] President Washington agreed. Western Pennsylvania, he told Hamilton on

*O*n the 6th of . . . September [1791] the person & property of Robert Johnson Collector of the Revenue for the Counties of Alleghany & Washington [were attacked]. A party of men armed and disguised way-laid him at a place on Pidgeon Creek in Washington county— seized tarred and feathered him cut off his hair and [took] his horse, obliging him to travel on foot a considerable distance in that . . . painful situation.[18]

In August 1794, Hamilton sent President Washington a report describing the rebellion in western Pennsylvania.

August 21, was engaged in "open rebellion."[19] Secretary of War Henry Knox was in Maine on personal business. As a result, Washington gave Hamilton orders to call to active duty twelve thousand militiamen from four states.

Marching Into Western Pennsylvania

On September 20, 1794, President Washington and Secretary Hamilton rode together out of Philadelphia. They journeyed west to join the troops gathering at Carlisle, Pennsylvania. They were determined to protect national authority.

Washington rode with the growing army to the foot of the Allegheny Mountains. He wished to show how important it was to restore order. But presidential duties finally called him back to Philadelphia. He left Governor Henry Lee of Virginia in command of the army. Hamilton remained to assist Lee in making military plans. The army made a four-week march west to Washington, Pennsylvania.

News of the approaching army frightened the rebellious farmers. Many of them boarded flatboats and escaped down the Ohio River. By the middle of November, hundreds of other Pennsylvania farmers had been caught and questioned. By that time, tax collectors were able to carry out their duties again. The Whiskey Rebellion had ended. On November 19, Hamilton wrote to President Washington that the army was returning eastward. One hundred fifty prisoners were brought back to Philadelphia for trial. Only two of these were found guilty of treason. President Washington granted them both pardons.

Resigning From Office

Soon after his return to Philadelphia, Hamilton sent the president his resignation as secretary of the treasury. He planned to leave office on January 31, 1795. Hamilton was tired. He complained of poor health. He wanted to return to New York City and private life.

Hamilton felt the American economy was now strong enough to allow him to retire. By 1795, the United States had the highest credit rating in Europe. European banks would now gladly loan the nation money. They knew they would be paid back with interest. Hamilton believed he had accomplished what needed to be done. The United States treasury was healthy and the economy was growing fast. President Washington paid Hamilton a high compliment, "My confidence in your talents, exertions, and integrity has been well placed."[20]

Citizen and General

"HAVING CONTRIBUTED to place [the economy] of the nation on a good footing," Hamilton wrote to his sister-in-law, Angelica Church, "I go to take a little care of my own."[1] By 1795, there were five Hamilton children: Philip, Angelica, Alexander, James, and John. Thirteen-year-old Philip was the oldest. John, the youngest, was two years old. In June 1795, the Hamilton family moved into a rented house at 63 Pine Street in New York City. Hamilton also used it as his law office.

After a hard day's work, Hamilton often painted watercolor pictures as a hobby. For fun, he also sometimes sang in the evenings with his daughter Angelica. She would play along on the piano or the harp. On Sunday afternoons, the Hamilton family often went walking along Broadway for exercise and pleasure.

Hamilton in Court

One night, a Frenchman visiting America passed Hamilton's house. Through the window, he was surprised to see Hamilton at his desk, writing by candlelight. "I have just come from viewing a man who had made the fortune of his country," the Frenchman marveled, "but now is working all night in order to support his family."[2]

Hamilton's law practice was busy and earned him money. His legal skills made him New York's leading lawyer. Hamilton wrote wills and contracts for clients. He presented cases in court. One major client was the United Insurance Company. The company insured sailing ships and their cargoes.

Hamilton and fellow lawyer Aaron Burr were involved together in one murder trial. They successfully defended Levi Weeks. Weeks was a carpenter accused of murdering Gulielma Sands. Her body was discovered at the bottom of a well. In the end, the jury found Weeks not guilty.

Public Scandal

Hamilton's affair with Maria Reynolds came back to haunt him in 1797. That summer, a series of pamphlets appeared in Philadelphia entitled "Historical Memoirs of the United States, for the Year 1796." They were written by James T. Callender. Two of the pamphlets revealed the Reynolds affair. Callender claimed the sex affair was only a story to hide the

Washington's Farewell Address

George Washington was determined to leave office at the end of his second term as president. He published a Farewell Address announcing his decision. It was Hamilton who wrote most of the document. He used ideas supplied by Washington and partly written by James Madison. It appeared in the *American Daily Advertiser*, a Philadelphia newspaper, on September 19, 1796. Walking down Broadway with his wife one day, Hamilton was offered a copy of the Farewell Address by a street vendor. "That man," Hamilton told his wife, "does not know he has asked me to purchase my own work."[3]

truth. Hamilton had really been involved in illegal bond trading with James Reynolds.

Years earlier, John Beckley had been clerk of the House of Representatives. Frederick Muhlenberg and Abraham Venable had given Beckley their notes on the Reynolds affair to make copies. It was believed Beckley made a copy for himself. Perhaps it had been Beckley who had given Callender his information.[4] Callender, a Democratic-Republican, clearly hoped to ruin the Federalist political leader Hamilton. Of his pamphlets, Callender wrote to Thomas Jefferson, "It is worth all that fifty of the best pens in America could have said against him."[5]

Hamilton realized he could no longer keep his affair with Maria Reynolds a secret. To defend his honest reputation as secretary of the treasury, Hamilton revealed his private shame. He published a ninety-five-page pamphlet. "The charge against me," he publicly declared, " . . . is a connection with one James Reynolds for purposes of improper pecuniary speculation. My real crime is an amorous connection with his wife."[6] The pamphlet revealed all of the embarrassing details of his sex affair with Maria Reynolds. "I have paid pretty severely for the folly," he admitted, "and can never recollect it without disgust and self-condemnation."[7] Betsy Hamilton forgave her husband for his hurtful behavior.

President John Adams

John Adams took office as second president of the United States on March 4, 1797. Although elected by the Federalist Party, Adams did not always follow their political ideals. He remained an independent thinker. Adams did not like Alexander Hamilton. He thought the Federalist leader was hungry for power. "I shall . . . maintain the same conduct toward him that I always did," Adams remarked, "—that is, to keep him at a distance."[8] But Hamilton had Federalist friends in the Adams Cabinet. They continued to ask Hamilton for political advice.

Since 1793, Great Britain and France had been at war. American merchant ships bound for Great Britain were sometimes seized or sunk by French warships. By the time Adams took office, America's relations with France were very bad. President Adams sent diplomats to France, but their peace mission failed. Before he would even agree to see them, French foreign minister Charles Maurice de Talleyrand-Perigord had three agents call upon the

Americans. The agents demanded a secret bribe of $250,000 for Talleyrand. The American diplomats angrily refused to pay. When Adams reported the scandal to Congress, the three French agents were given the names X, Y, and Z.

The "XYZ Affair" outraged most Americans. They insisted the country prepare to fight. Congress passed laws to strengthen United States military forces. Hamilton agreed that America needed to "take vigorous and comprehensive measures of defense."[9] The

Although elected by the Federalist political party, President John Adams was an independent thinker.

undeclared war against France came to be called the Quasi-War, or Half-War.

A New Army

"Mr. Secretary," asked President Adams in 1798, "whom shall we appoint Commander-in-Chief?" Secretary of State Timothy Pickering quickly replied, "Colonel Hamilton." "Oh no!" Adams exclaimed, "it is not his turn by a great deal."[10] In the end, Adams sent a letter to George Washington. He asked Washington to come out of retirement. The nation needed him once more to lead its army.

Washington agreed to take charge if the country were actually invaded. He suggested that Alexander Hamilton be his second-in-command with the rank of major general. Secretary of War James McHenry and

Secretary of State Pickering strongly supported the idea. As loyal Federalists, McHenry and Pickering saw this as a chance to make Hamilton more powerful.

On September 25, 1798, Adams reluctantly accepted Washington's choice of Hamilton. But he privately complained that Washington had forced him to approve "the most restless, impatient . . . and unprincipled [schemer] in the United States, if not the world, to be second in command . . . "[11]

Hamilton swiftly took up the work of enlisting an army of 12,500 new troops. He took an interest in all the details of preparing the new army. He designed uniforms and outlined military routine. He also suggested the establishment of a military academy for army officers at West Point, New York. Washington and others had promoted this idea, too. In time, Congress passed a bill creating the United States Military Academy. The military academy was founded at West Point in 1802.

Adams Makes a Bold Decision

On February 18, 1799, President Adams suddenly announced his decision to send William Vans Murray as a special diplomat to France. Adams hoped to improve relations between the two nations. Hamilton and many Federalists in Congress were surprised and disappointed. Oliver Ellsworth and William Davie later joined Vans Murray on the American peace mission. If their efforts were successful, it would ruin the Federalist Party's desire for war with France. In the war between France and Great Britain, the Federalists had always favored Great Britain.

On December 14, 1799, sixty-seven-year-old George Washington died of pneumonia at his Virginia estate, Mount Vernon. Hamilton joined in the national mourning. Washington had been a great influence and help in Hamilton's career. "I have been much indebted to the kindness of the General . . . " Hamilton admitted.[12] With Washington's death, it appeared that Hamilton had become the highest-ranking officer in the army.

In November 1800, news from France at last arrived. President Adams's diplomats had succeeded. A new peace treaty with France had been signed. The Quasi-War was over. Peace with France ended Hamilton's career as a general. President Adams ordered the militia disbanded and sent home. Hamilton closed his military headquarters in New York City and retired from military service.

New York Politics

New York's state elections took place in April 1800. The newly elected members of the state legislature would have an important duty. They would cast New York's electoral votes for president in the national election that fall. Hamilton campaigned hard for Federalist candidates to win seats in the legislature. "Every day he is seen in the streets," declared one newspaper, "hurrying this way, and darting that."[13]

The Democratic-Republicans in New York were led by Aaron Burr. Burr proved an even better campaigner than Hamilton. Burr kept files on every voter in town. He was able to give voters personal attention. Burr sent German-speaking Democratic-Republicans to campaign in New York City's German neighborhoods. He also kept an open house for Democratic-Republican campaigners. Tables were crowded with drinks and food. The house had sleeping rooms with mattresses on the floors. Campaign workers could rest there when tired. On election day, the Democratic-Republicans won the most seats in the legislature. Hamilton bitterly felt he was losing political control of New York because of Aaron Burr.

The Election of 1800

In the national election of 1800, Democratic-Republicans picked Thomas Jefferson to run for president against John Adams. To gain support in the North, they chose Aaron Burr to be his running mate. The Federalists selected Charles Cotesworth Pinckney to be Adams's running mate. Adams was not well-liked by many Federalists. Hamilton especially did not like him.

John Adams had always resented Hamilton's influence on his Cabinet officers. In May 1800, Adams finally forced Timothy Pickering, his secretary of state, and James McHenry, his secretary of war, out of office. Adams regarded them as "Hamilton's spies."[14] Hamilton responded by angrily calling Adams "a mere old woman and unfit for President."[15]

In the presidential campaign, Adams received little support from Hamilton's Federalist followers. Hamilton believed that Adams was even worse than Jefferson. "If we must have an enemy at the head of the Government," Hamilton told fellow Federalists, "let it be one whom we can oppose, and for whom we are not responsible."[16] Hamilton even had a fifty-four-page pamphlet printed. It was entitled "A Letter from Alexander Hamilton Concerning the Public Conduct and Character of John Adams, Esq., President of the United States." The pamphlet openly attacked Adams. Hamilton accused Adams of vanity, jealousy, and a very bad temper. He sent the pamphlet to two hundred Federalist leaders. But Aaron Burr got hold of a copy and had it widely published. Democratic-Republicans were thrilled to discover Hamilton's hatred of Adams had split the Federalist Party.

The Tie Vote

On February 11, 1801, the official results of the presidential election were announced. Jefferson received 73 electoral votes, Adams 65, and Pinckney 64. But in a surprise twist, Jefferson's running mate Aaron Burr also received 73 votes. All of the Democratic-Republican electors had given their second votes to Burr. As a result, Burr had tied with Jefferson. The election, according to the Constitution, would have to be decided in the House of Representatives.

Members of the House immediately began the balloting process to choose which of the two would be the president. Each of the sixteen states had one vote. If the votes of a state's representatives were evenly split, the state was to cast a blank ballot. Many Federalist congressmen favored Aaron Burr simply because they disliked Jefferson so much. On the first ballot, Jefferson failed to get the nine votes necessary to win the election. Eight states voted for him and six for Burr. The other two were evenly divided and did not vote.

Tension over the Jefferson-Burr deadlock increased during the next six days of balloting. Jefferson had been the Democratic-Republican's candidate for president. But Burr refused to give up the chance to grab the office. It was whispered that Burr was secretly bargaining with the Federalists for votes.[17]

Hamilton hated both men. But in the end, he threw his support behind Jefferson. "Mr. Jefferson, though too revolutionary in his notions, is yet a lover of liberty . . . " Hamilton exclaimed, "[while] Mr. Burr loves nothing but himself. . . . In the choice of evils. . . . Jefferson is in my view less dangerous than Burr."[18] Hamilton sent dozens of letters urging Federalists to support Jefferson. To Gouverneur Morris, Hamilton wrote, "If there be a man in the world I ought to hate, it is Jefferson. With Burr I have always been personally well. But the public good must be paramount to every private consideration."[19]

This is a portrait of Democratic-Republican politician Aaron Burr. For years, Hamilton and Burr struggled for political control of New York.

On February 17, on the thirty-sixth ballot, Jefferson finally obtained the votes of nine states. On March 4, he took the oath of office as third president of the United States in Washington, D.C. Aaron Burr became vice

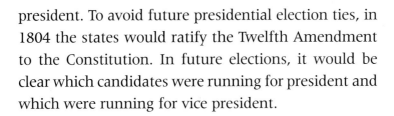

president. To avoid future presidential election ties, in 1804 the states would ratify the Twelfth Amendment to the Constitution. In future elections, it would be clear which candidates were running for president and which were running for vice president.

A Family Tragedy

Hamilton and other partners established a new newspaper, the *New York Evening Post*, in November 1801. William Coleman became its editor. Hamilton sometimes contributed articles. As Coleman remarked, "he always keeps himself minutely informed on all political matters."[20] Today, New Yorkers can still buy the *New York Evening Post* at newsstands.

In its eighth issue, the *New York Evening Post* reported tragic news. It told the history of a duel involving Hamilton's twenty-year-old son Philip. Philip Hamilton had read a speech given by Democratic-Republican George I. Eacker. The speech had attacked the Federalist Party. On November 20, 1801, Philip Hamilton and a friend named Price happened to share a theater box occupied by Eacker and friends. Philip in loud conversation made rude remarks about Eacker's speech. Eacker held his temper until after the show. In the theatre lobby, he insulted Philip Hamilton and Price. In response, both young men challenged Eacker to duels.

Dueling, with pistols or swords, was considered the thing to do when one's honor was questioned. It was the way many gentlemen settled personal arguments in those days. But dueling was illegal in New York.

To escape New York laws, duelists often crossed the Hudson River to New Jersey to fight.

Eacker met with Price on November 22. On the day of their duel, they exchanged four shots. Neither was hit by a bullet, and the two men declared themselves satisfied. The next day, Eacker faced Philip Hamilton. Both men raised their weapons at the same moment. Eacker's shot tore through Philip Hamilton's body and ended up in his left arm. The young man fell without having fired his pistol. He lived for fourteen hours, but died at home in the afternoon of November 23.

Alexander Hamilton was stunned by his son's violent death. Some friends thought the terrible tragedy changed Hamilton's outlook on life. "Never did I see a man so completely overwhelmed with grief as Hamilton has been," Robert Troup noted soon after the duel.[21] Hamilton seemed never to recover from his feeling of sadness. By the end of 1801, his power as leader of the Federalist Party was already fading. Now, in losing his oldest son, he seemed to have lost his will to live. "What can I do better than withdraw from the Scene?" he wrote Gouverneur Morris in February 1802. "Every day proves to me more and more, that this American world was not for me."[22] On June 2, Betsy Hamilton gave birth to the Hamilton's last child. They named the baby boy Philip, in honor of his dead brother.

The Grange

Even before the death of his son, Hamilton had decided to retire from politics. He had bought thirty-two acres of land. It overlooked the Hudson

Hamilton's home, "The Grange," is shown in this picture. The Hamilton family moved into the house in August 1802. It still stands today on Convent Avenue in the Harlem section of New York City.

River in the section of Manhattan that is today Harlem. In 1802, it was open countryside several miles north of New York City. The two-story house Hamilton built had porches on the north and south sides. He called the house "The Grange." It was the same name as the mansion of his royal Hamilton relatives in Scotland.

As the city has grown around it, the house has been moved a couple of blocks from its first site. (Today, The Grange stands on Convent Avenue above 141st Street.) The Hamilton family moved into the new house in August 1802.

The Duel at Weehawken

AS HIS FOUR-YEAR TERM as vice president neared its end, Aaron Burr realized he must find a new political office. The Democratic-Republicans would not chose him to be vice presidential candidate again. In February 1804, Burr gathered the support of enough New York Democratic-Republicans and Federalists to make a campaign for governor. In a switch, Hamilton threw his support behind Democratic-Republican candidate Morgan Lewis. In April, Burr lost the election to Lewis by a vote of 30,829 to 22,139. Burr blamed Hamilton's influence for his failure to become governor. It seemed Aaron Burr, the vice president of the United States, and Alexander Hamilton, the former secretary of the treasury, were determined to oppose one another.

The Challenge

After the election for governor, a newspaper article appeared in the *Albany Register*. It was written by Dr. Charles D. Cooper. In it, Cooper stated that he had heard Hamilton say that he "looked upon Mr. Burr to be a dangerous man, and one who ought not to be trusted with the reins of government." Cooper also wrote, "I could detail to you a still more despicable opinion which General HAMILTON has expressed of Mr. BURR."[1]

On June 18, 1804, Burr sent a friend, William van Ness, to visit Hamilton. Van Ness brought with him a copy of Cooper's news-paper article and a note from Burr demanding an explanation. During the next nine days, several letters passed back and forth between Hamilton and Burr. Burr ended up demanding a general apology for whatever Hamilton may have said. For his part, Hamilton believed he was entitled to his opinions.

In June 1804, Alexander Hamilton accepted Aaron Burr's challenge to a duel. Hamilton, pictured here, was against dueling, but his sense of honor demanded that he meet Burr.

Burr finally challenged Hamilton to a duel on June 27. Hamilton had cases in court that he felt it his duty to complete. He also wanted time to put his personal affairs in order. But he agreed to meet Burr on July 11 at Weehawken, New Jersey. Weehawken was a popular dueling ground across the Hudson River. It was the place where Philip Hamilton had been killed.

Making Preparations

In the days before the duel, Hamilton attended to his law work. He also wrote his will and two letters to his wife. They were to be delivered to her if he were killed. In a note to his friend Nathaniel Pendleton, however, Hamilton condemned dueling. He told Pendleton he would meet Burr, but he would not fire his pistol at him. "I have resolved," he wrote, " . . . to reserve and throw away my first fire . . . thus giving [an] opportunity to Col. Burr to pause and to reflect."[2] Years earlier, Hamilton had written to Dr. William Gordon, "To prove your own innocence, or the malice of an accuser, the worst method you can take is to run him through the body or shoot him through the head."[3]

On the Fourth of July, Hamilton attended a New York City meeting of the Society of the Cincinnati. He was president of that organization of Revolutionary War officers. During the dinner, he saluted guests with a song. Aaron Burr was attending the dinner, too. Witnesses said Burr watched Hamilton closely while he sang.

The Fateful Meeting

The morning of July 11, 1804, was hot and hazy. At five o'clock, Hamilton boarded a rowboat in Manhattan. His friend Pendleton was with him.

The Society of the Cincinnati

At the end of the Revolutionary War, American army officers formed a social group to be called the Society of the Cincinnati. The society was named after the Roman general Lucius Quinctus Cincinnatus. After faithful service in the army, Cincinnatus had returned to peaceful civilian life. These American soldiers hoped to do the same. George Washington was elected the first president of the society. Alexander Hamilton became the second. The society still survives today. Its members are descendants of the society's first members.

Pendleton would act as his second in the duel. A second acted as a duelist's witness and representative. It was his duty to see that the duel was fought correctly. Hamilton's personal doctor, David Hosack, and two oarsmen were also aboard. The group rowed across the Hudson River to Weehawken. On the New Jersey side of the river are high rocky cliffs called the Palisades. The well-known dueling ground was on a narrow ledge located near the shore. It was only about ten feet wide and forty feet long.

When they reached the shore, Hosack and the oarsmen were asked to remain behind at the boat. Because dueling was illegal, neither of the duelists wished more witnesses than necessary. Burr and his second, William van Ness, were already on the dueling ground. Under his arm, Pendleton carried a box containing two .56 caliber pistols. The distance agreed upon between the two duelists was ten paces—about twenty feet. The seconds loaded the

My dear Eliza—This letter, my very dear Eliza, will not be delivered to you, unless I shall first have terminated my earthly career. . . . If it had been possible for me to have avoided the interview, my love for you and my precious children would have been alone a decisive motive. But it was not possible, without sacrifices which would have rendered me unworthy of your esteem. I need not tell you of the pangs I feel, from the idea of quitting you. . . . The consolations of Religion, my beloved, can alone support you. . . . Fly to the bosom of your God and be comforted. With my last idea; I shall cherish the sweet hope of meeting you in a better world. Adieu, best of wives and best of Women. Embrace all my darling Children for me. Ever Yours, AH[4]

One week before his duel with Burr, Hamilton wrote this letter to his wife. He left it for her to read if he were killed.

pistols and ten paces were stepped off and marked. It was agreed Pendleton would call out "Present" as the signal to fire.

It was about seven o'clock when Hamilton and Burr took their positions opposite one another. Just before the final command, Hamilton asked for a brief delay. He took his eyeglasses out of his coat pocket. He put them on and squinted into the sunshine.

Alexander Hamilton and Aaron Burr dueled at Weehawken, New Jersey, on July 11, 1804.

He raised his pistol, pointed it at several imaginary targets, and at last said he was ready.

Out of the quiet, Pendleton suddenly called out the fateful word "Present." The noise of two gunshots cracked through the air. It sounded as if they had been fired at nearly the same moment. Pendleton later claimed Hamilton's shot was fired only as a painful reflex action. He insisted Hamilton's bullet went high into the air, cutting a branch from a cedar tree.

Aaron Burr's bullet, however, hit its mark. It struck Hamilton in the right side, throwing him off his feet. Hamilton turned to his left and fell on his face. Burr seemed surprised and saddened to see Hamilton fall. He started toward Hamilton, but Van Ness took him by the arm. He hurried Burr toward their boat and away.

Hosack heard the sound of the gunshots. He rushed to the scene to offer Hamilton medical aid. "I found him half sitting on the ground, supported in the arms of Mr. Pendleton," Hosack recalled. "His countenance of death I shall never forget."[5] Hamilton was only able to say, "This is a mortal wound, Doctor," before he fell into unconsciousness.[6]

Pendleton and Hosack carried Hamilton down to their boat. While crossing the Hudson River, Hamilton regained his senses long enough to mutter to Hosack, "Pendleton knows I did not mean to fire at Colonel Burr ... "[7] About fifty yards from the Manhattan shore, Hamilton opened his eyes again. "Let Mrs. Hamilton be immediately sent for," he sighed. "Let the event be gradually broken to her; but give her hopes."[8]

The Death Watch

The boat docked at the foot of Horatio Street in Greenwich Village. Hamilton was carried to the nearby home of William Bayard, an old friend and legal client. Although Dr. Hosack gave him medicine to relieve him, Hamilton was in great pain. "I had not the shadow of a hope of his recovery," the doctor later remarked.[9] Other doctors were called to examine the wounded man. They discovered Burr's bullet had cut through Hamilton's liver and ended up lodged in his spine. He could not survive such a terrible injury.

In time, Betsy Hamilton arrived from The Grange. She learned for the first time what had happened to her husband. During the next hours, she remained at his bedside. At one point, their seven children were brought into the room. Dr. Hosack recalled Hamilton "opened his eyes, gave them one look, and closed them again, till they were taken away."[10] During the night, newspaper editor William Coleman heard him sigh, "My beloved wife and children."[11]

Several other people gathered by Hamilton's deathbed. Oliver Wolcott was there, and so was Episcopal bishop Benjamin Moore. Finally, at two o'clock on the afternoon of July 12, 1804, forty-nine-year-old Alexander Hamilton died. Bishop Moore remarked, "Death closed the awful scene. He [died] without a struggle, and almost without a groan."[12] Wolcott later commented, "Thus has [died] one of the greatest men of this or any age."[13]

Funeral of a Patriot

"When a great man falls, his nation mourns," exclaimed the *United States Gazette* of Hamilton's tragic death.[14] Hamilton's funeral was on July 14. New York City declared the day an official day of mourning. Church bells tolled, and British and French warships in the harbor fired their cannons. Flags were flown at half-mast. The funeral parade began a long march from the house of Hamilton's brother-in-law, John Church, to Trinity Church on Broadway. "The streets were lined with people," described William Coleman, "doors and windows were filled, [mostly] with weeping females, and even the housetops were covered with spectators."[15]

It was a military funeral. Soldiers and drummers marched behind the carriage that slowly carried the coffin. Betsy Hamilton and her children followed. New York politicians, students and professors of Columbia College, bankers, army and navy officers, religious leaders, and foreign diplomats all solemnly marched behind. In the churchyard of Trinity Church, the coffin was lowered into the ground. Throughout the day, the church bells continued to ring. There had not been so much grief in New York since the death of Washington.

The End of Aaron Burr

The bullet that killed Alexander Hamilton ended Aaron Burr's career as a politician. "All office, public honors, power, and trust, are now forever out of the reach of Aaron Burr!" exclaimed the *Albany Centinel*.[16] After the duel, Burr fled New York City. For a time, he

Trinity Churchyard and September 11

Visitors to Trinity Church today can still see Alexander Hamilton's grave. Famous steamboat inventor Robert Fulton and General Horatio Gates, the hero of the Battle of Saratoga, are also buried in the churchyard. Trinity Church stood only two blocks away from the twin towers of the World Trade Center. The towers were destroyed by terrorists on September 11, 2001. Bits of metal, stone, and clouds of dust showered down on little Trinity Church. However, the church and its cemetery were undamaged.

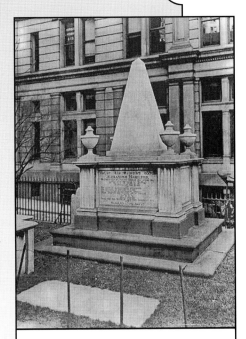

This is a view of Alexander Hamilton's grave in Trinity Churchyard in New York City.

was wanted for the crimes of dueling and murder. But the charges were later dropped.

Burr was later charged with treason. There was a rumor he had schemed to form an independent empire in the Louisiana Territory. He eventually was found not guilty in 1807. After living for years in Europe, Burr continued to practice law in New York. But few people would visit with him socially. He died in 1836.

Lasting Gifts of a Founding Father

Elizabeth Hamilton lived a long life and died at the age of ninety-seven in 1854. "Never forget," she once told a visiting historian, "that my husband made your government."[17] It is certainly true that Alexander Hamilton did much to help make the United States the nation it is today. All through his adult life, he gave the country brave and brilliant service as a soldier and a statesman. His total sense of patriotism has easily won him a place among America's founding fathers.

The United States could not have won its independence from Great Britain without dedicated soldiers like Hamilton. During the Revolutionary War, he showed courage on the battlefield. As a staff officer at Washington's headquarters, he did years of valuable duty.

When the fighting was over, Hamilton plunged into the work of making the United States a successful nation. He became a member of Congress and delegate to the Annapolis and Constitutional conventions. He understood the direction the country needed to take. He proudly signed the new Constitution and worked hard to get it ratified. His contributions to *The Federalist* supporting the Constitution are still regarded highly.

George Washington wisely chose Hamilton to be the first secretary of the treasury. As treasury secretary, Hamilton was able to turn bold economic ideas into reality. Under his guiding hand, the United States changed from a weak nation in debt into a thriving nation with a hopeful future. Looking back, it seems impossible that one person could have achieved so much. "The American world was not made for me," Hamilton once said in a moment of discouragement. He could not have been more wrong. As one of our founding fathers, Alexander Hamilton helped make the United States into a great country.

Timeline

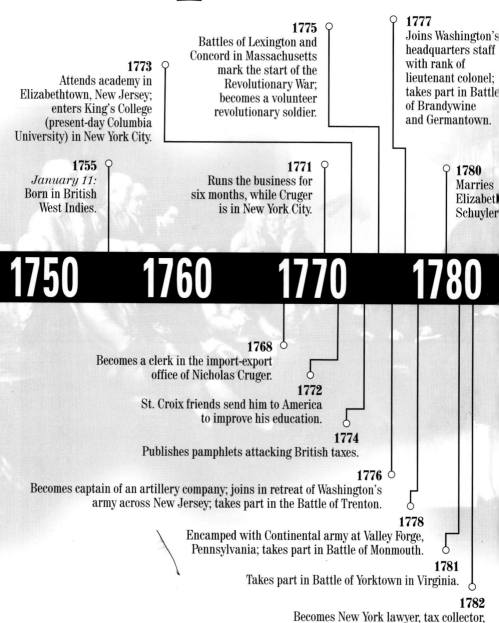

1773
Attends academy in Elizabethtown, New Jersey; enters King's College (present-day Columbia University) in New York City.

1775
Battles of Lexington and Concord in Massachusetts mark the start of the Revolutionary War; becomes a volunteer revolutionary soldier.

1777
Joins Washington's headquarters staff with rank of lieutenant colonel; takes part in Battle of Brandywine and Germantown.

1755
January 11: Born in British West Indies.

1771
Runs the business for six months, while Cruger is in New York City.

1780
Marries Elizabeth Schuyler

1750   1760   1770   1780

1768
Becomes a clerk in the import-export office of Nicholas Cruger.

1772
St. Croix friends send him to America to improve his education.

1774
Publishes pamphlets attacking British taxes.

1776
Becomes captain of an artillery company; joins in retreat of Washington's army across New Jersey; takes part in the Battle of Trenton.

1778
Encamped with Continental army at Valley Forge, Pennsylvania; takes part in Battle of Monmouth.

1781
Takes part in Battle of Yorktown in Virginia.

1782
Becomes New York lawyer, tax collector, and delegate to Continental Congress.

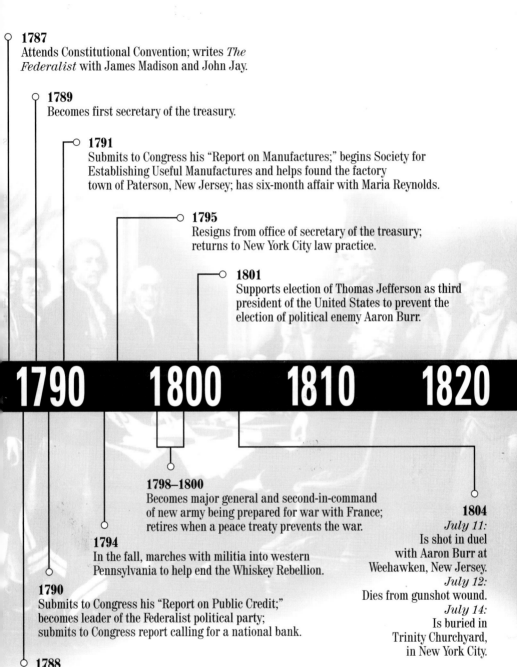

1787
Attends Constitutional Convention; writes *The Federalist* with James Madison and John Jay.

1789
Becomes first secretary of the treasury.

1791
Submits to Congress his "Report on Manufactures;" begins Society for Establishing Useful Manufactures and helps found the factory town of Paterson, New Jersey; has six-month affair with Maria Reynolds.

1795
Resigns from office of secretary of the treasury; returns to New York City law practice.

1801
Supports election of Thomas Jefferson as third president of the United States to prevent the election of political enemy Aaron Burr.

1790 1800 1810 1820

1798–1800
Becomes major general and second-in-command of new army being prepared for war with France; retires when a peace treaty prevents the war.

1804
July 11:
Is shot in duel with Aaron Burr at Weehawken, New Jersey.
July 12:
Dies from gunshot wound.
July 14:
Is buried in Trinity Churchyard, in New York City.

1794
In the fall, marches with militia into western Pennsylvania to help end the Whiskey Rebellion.

1790
Submits to Congress his "Report on Public Credit;" becomes leader of the Federalist political party; submits to Congress report calling for a national bank.

1788
Attends New York ratification convention and helps persuade delegates to accept the Constitution.

1786
Attends Annapolis Convention.

Chapter Notes

Chapter 1. The Fight for the Constitution

1. Jacob Ernest Cooke, *Alexander Hamilton* (New York: Charles Scribner's Sons, 1982), p. 60.

2. Broadus Mitchell, *Alexander Hamilton* (New York: Oxford University Press, 1976), p. 167.

3. Louis M. Hacker, *Alexander Hamilton in the American Tradition* (Westport, Conn.: Greenwood Press, Publishers, 1957), p. 124.

4. Milton Lomask, *Odd Destiny: A Life of Alexander Hamilton* (New York: Farrar, Straus & Giroux, 1969), p. 99.

5. Ibid., p. 100.

6. Richard Brookhiser, *Alexander Hamilton, American* (New York: The Free Press, 1999), p. 74.

7. Cooke, p. 65.

Chapter 2. Boyhood in the West Indies

1. Dorothie Bobbe, "The Boyhood of Alexander Hamilton," *American Heritage*, June 1955, p. 6.

2. Ibid.

3. Jacob Ernest Cooke, *Alexander Hamilton* (New York: Charles Scribner's Sons, 1982), p. 1.

4. James Thomas Flexner, *The Young Hamilton* (Boston: Little, Brown and Company, 1978), p. 18.

5. Cooke, p. 2.

6. Flexner, p. 21.

7. Ibid., p. 25.

8. Richard Brookhiser, *Alexander Hamilton, American* (New York: The Free Press, 1999), p. 17.

9. Cooke, p. 4.

10. Broadus Mitchell, *Alexander Hamilton* (New York: Oxford University Press, 1976), p. 13.

11. Ibid., p. 14.

12. Ibid., p. 15.

13. Ibid., p. 17.

14. Milton Lomask, *Odd Destiny: A Life of Alexander Hamilton* (New York: Farrar, Straus & Giroux, 1969), p. 13.

15. Flexner, p. 50.

Chapter 3. Young Revolutionary

1. Richard Brookhiser, *Alexander Hamilton, American* (New York: The Free Press, 1999), p. 21.

2. James Thomas Flexner, *The Young Hamilton* (Boston: Little, Brown and Company, 1978), p. 67.

3. Ibid., p. 73.

4. Brookhiser, p. 25.

5. Broadus Mitchell, *Alexander Hamilton* (New York: Oxford University Press, 1976), pp. 28–29.

6. Brookhiser, p. 26.

7. Milton Lomask, *Odd Destiny: A Life of Alexander Hamilton* (New York: Farrar, Straus & Giroux, 1969), p. 38.

8. Flexner, p. 123.

9. Mitchell, p. 36.

10. Flexner, p. 129.

Chapter 4. Lieutenant Colonel Hamilton

1. Jacob Ernest Cooke, *Alexander Hamilton* (New York: Charles Scribner's Sons, 1982), p. 14.

2. Ibid.

3. James Thomas Flexner, *The Young Hamilton* (Boston: Little, Brown and Company, 1978), p. 146.

4. Flexner, p. 158.

5. Broadus Mitchell, *Alexander Hamilton* (New York: Oxford University Press, 1976), pp. 42–43.

6. Cooke, p. 17.

7. Milton Lomask, *Odd Destiny: A Life of Alexander Hamilton* (New York: Farrar, Straus & Giroux, 1969), p. 48.

8. Ibid.

9. Flexner, p. 172.

10. Mitchell, pp. 45–46.

11. Flexner, p. 205.

Chapter 5. From Valley Forge to Yorktown

1. James Thomas Flexner, *The Young Hamilton* (Boston: Little, Brown and Company, 1978), p. 207.

2. George F. Scheer and Hugh F. Rankin, *Rebels and Redcoats* (New York: New American Library, 1957), p. 332.

3. Richard Brookhiser, *Alexander Hamilton, American* (New York: The Free Press, 1999), p. 35.

4. Broadus Mitchell, *Alexander Hamilton* (New York: Oxford University Press, 1976), p. 63.

5. Flexner, p. 277.

6. Ibid., pp. 271–272.

7. Milton Lomask, *Odd Destiny: A Life of Alexander Hamilton* (New York: Farrar, Straus & Giroux, 1969), p. 66.

8. Broadus Mitchell, *Alexander Hamilton: Youth to Maturity, 1755–1788* (New York: The Macmillan Company, 1957), p. 204.

9. Flexner, p. 308.

10. Ibid., p. 309.

11. Ibid., p. 315.

12. Ibid., p. 314.

13. Mitchell, *Alexander Hamilton*, p. 77.

14. Louis M. Hacker, *Alexander Hamilton in the American Tradition* (Westport, Conn.: Greenwood Press, Publishers, 1957), p. 222.

15. Flexner, p. 219.

16. Lomask, p. 73.

17. Jacob Ernest Cooke, *Alexander Hamilton* (New York: Charles Scribner's Sons, 1982), p. 27.

18. Flexner, p. 351.

19. Mitchell, *Alexander Hamilton*, p. 101.

20. Flexner, p. 365.

21. Ibid., p. 367.

Chapter 6. Lawyer and Congressman

1. Milton Lomask, *Odd Destiny: A Life of Alexander Hamilton* (New York: Farrar, Straus & Giroux, 1969), p. 79.

2. Broadus Mitchell, *Alexander Hamilton* (New York: Oxford University Press, 1976), p. 106.

3. James Thomas Flexner, *The Young Hamilton* (Boston: Little, Brown and Company, 1978), p. 374.

4. Ibid., p. 375.

5. Mitchell, p. 107.

6. Richard Brookhiser, *Alexander Hamilton, American* (New York: The Free Press, 1999), pp. 54–55.

7. Flexner, p. 389.

8. Mitchell, p. 128.

9. Flexner, p. 431.

10. Louis M. Hacker, *Alexander Hamilton in the American Tradition* (Westport, Conn.: Greenwood Press, Publisher, 1957), p. 77.

11. Brookhiser, p. 58.

12. Hacker, p. 106.

Chapter 7. A New National Government

1. Broadus Mitchell, *Alexander Hamilton* (New York: Oxford University Press, 1976), p. 152.

2. Ibid.

3. Jacob Ernest Cooke, *Alexander Hamilton* (New York: Charles Scribner's Sons, 1982), p. 51.

4. Richard Brookhiser, *Alexander Hamilton, American* (New York: The Free Press, 1999), p. 65.

5. Mitchell, p. 155.

6. Catherine Drinker Bowen, *Miracle at Philadelphia* (Boston: Little, Brown and Company, 1966), p. 201.

7. Brookhiser, p. 67.

8. Bowen, p. 256.

9. Milton Lomask, *Odd Destiny: A Life of Alexander Hamilton* (New York: Farrar, Straus & Giroux, 1969), p. 92.

10. Bowen, p. 213.

11. Garry Wills, *James Madison* (New York: Times Books, Henry Holt and Company, 2002), p. 30.

12. Louis M. Hacker, *Alexander Hamilton in the American Tradition* (Westport, Conn.: Greenwood Press, Publishers, 1957), p. 120.

13. William F. Swindler, "The Letters of Publius," *American Heritage*, June 1961, p. 92.

14. John Bartlett, *Familiar Quotations* (Boston: Little, Brown and Company, 1992), p. 355.

15. Swindler, p. 96.

16. Brookhiser, p. 72.

Chapter 8. Secretary of the Treasury

1. Broadus Mitchell, *Alexander Hamilton* (New York: Oxford University Press, 1976), p. 179.

2. Jacob Ernest Cooke, *Alexander Hamilton* (New York: Charles Scribner's Sons, 1982), p. 73.

3. Louis M. Hacker, *Alexander Hamilton in the American Tradition* (Westport, Conn.: Greenwood Press, Publishers, 1957), p. 134.

4. Mitchell, p. 200.

5. Robert C. Alberts, "The Cantankerous Mr. Maclay," *American Heritage*, October 1974, p. 50.

6. Cooke, p. 91.

7. James R. Webb, "The Fateful Encounter," *American Heritage*, August 1975, p. 47.

8. Richard Brookhiser, *Alexander Hamilton, American* (New York: The Free Press, 1999), p. 104.

9. Ibid., p. 93.

10. Ibid., p. 94.

11. Ibid., p. 95.

12. Brookhiser, pp. 97–98.

13. Hacker, pp. 184–185.

14. Robert C. Alberts, "The Notorious Affair of Mrs. Reynolds," *American Heritage*, February 1973, p. 9.

15. Ibid., p. 11.

16. Ibid.

17. Brookhiser, pp. 118–119.

18. Harold C. Syrett, ed., *The Papers of Alexander Hamilton* (New York: Columbia University Press, 1972), vol. XVII, p. 32.

19. Cooke, p. 151.

20. Mitchell, p. 303.

Chapter 9. Citizen and General

1. Jacob Ernest Cooke, *Alexander Hamilton* (New York: Charles Scribner's Sons, 1982), p. 158.

2. Richard Brookhiser, *Alexander Hamilton, American* (New York: The Free Press, 1999), p. 121.

3. Ibid., p. 128.

4. Broadus Mitchell, *Alexander Hamilton* (New York: Oxford University Press, 1976), p. 328.

5. Robert C. Alberts, "The Notorious Affair of Mrs. Reynolds," *American Heritage*, February 1973, p. 91.

6. Brookhiser, p. 133.

7. Ibid., p. 134.

8. Cooke, p. 176.

9. Ibid., p. 190.

10. Milton Lomask, *Odd Destiny: A Life of Alexander Hamilton* (New York: Farrar, Straus & Giroux, 1969), p. 151.

11. James R. Webb, "The Fateful Encounter," *American Heritage*, August 1975, p. 47.

12. Mitchell, p. 342.

13. Brookhiser, p. 147.

14. Louis M. Hacker, *Alexander Hamilton in the American Tradition* (Westport, Conn.: Greenwood Press, Publishers, 1957), p. 233.

15. Francis Russell, *Adams An American Dynasty* (New York: American Heritage Publishing Co., Inc., 1976), p. 126.

16. Paul F. Boller, Jr., *Presidential Campaigns* (New York: Oxford University Press, 1984), pp. 10–11.

17. David McCullough, *John Adams* (New York: Simon & Schuster, 2001), pp. 557–558.

18. Ibid.

19. Hacker, p. 234.

20. Cooke, p. 233.

21. Ibid., p. 232.

22. Mitchell, p. 358.

Chapter 10. The Duel at Weehawken

1. Jacob Ernest Cooke, *Alexander Hamilton* (New York: Charles Scribner's Sons, 1982), p. 239.

2. Joseph J. Ellis, *Founding Brothers* (New York: Alfred A. Knopf, 2001), p. 23.

3. Broadus Mitchell, *Alexander Hamilton* (New York: Oxford University Press, 1976), p. 371.

4. Andrew Carroll, ed., *Letters of a Nation* (New York: Kodansha International, 1997), pp. 360–361.

5. Cooke, p. 242.

6. Ellis, p. 25.

7. Ibid., p. 26.

8. James R. Webb, "The Fateful Encounter," *American Heritage*, August 1975, p. 92.

9. Richard Brookhiser, *Alexander Hamilton, American* (New York: The Free Press, 1999), p. 212.

10. Cooke, p. 242.

11. William Coleman, *A Collection of the Facts and Documents, Relative to the Death of Major-General Alexander Hamilton* (Freeport, N.Y.: Books For Libraries Press, 1969), p. 22.

12. Cooke, p. 243.

13. Brookhiser, p. 213.

14. Coleman, p. 79.

15. Ibid., p. 42.

16. Ibid., p. 192.

17. Milton Lomask, *Odd Destiny: A Life of Alexander Hamilton* (New York: Farrar, Straus & Giroux, 1969), pp. 171–172.

Glossary

ambition—A desire to better oneself.

apprentice—One bound to serve another in order to learn an art or trade.

ballot—A secret vote or a piece of paper on which a vote is written.

bankrupt—Reduced to a condition of debt or ruin.

battalion—A body of organized military troops, usually larger than a company and smaller than a division.

bayonet—A pointed or bladelike steel weapon attached at the end of a musket or rifle.

bond—A certificate that promises a future value and pays regular interest.

charter—A grant of rights or privileges.

customs—Taxes on imported or exported goods.

delegate—A representative to a convention or conference.

economics—The study of the exchange of goods and services for profit; the management of money.

federal—Relating to a central or national government.

illegitimate—Not recognized as a lawful child; born of parents not married to each other.

legislature—A body of people having the power to make laws.

militia—An armed force usually only called to duty during an emergency.

musket—A gun with a long barrel that is smooth inside.

pneumonia—A disease of the lungs.

ratify—To approve formally.

Further Reading

Books

Clark, Charles. *Patriots of the Revolutionary War*. San Diego, Calif.: Lucent Books, 2003.

Jaffe, Steven H. *Who Were the Founding Fathers?: Two Hundred Years of Reinventing American History*. New York: H. Holt and Co., 1996.

Jones, Veda Boyd. *Alexander Hamilton*. Broomall, Pa.: Chelsea House, 1999.

Kallen, Stuart A. *Alexander Hamilton*. Minneapolis, Minn.: ABDO Publishing Co., 2002.

Lucas, Eileen. *The Aaron Burr Treason Trial*. Berkeley Heights, N.J.: Enslow Publishers, Inc., 2003.

Lukes, Bonnie. *The American Revolution*. San Diego, Calif.: Lucent Books, 1996.

Stein, R. Conrad. *Valley Forge*. Danbury, Conn.: Childrens Press, 1999.

Weidner, Daniel, Ed.D. *The Constitution: The Preamble and the Articles*. Berkeley Heights, N.J.: Enslow Publishers, Inc., 2002.

Internet Addresses

"Alexander Hamilton, New York." *NARA Exhibit Hall. The Founding Fathers: New York.* n.d. <http://www.archives.gov/exhibit_hall/charters_of_freedom/constitution/new_york.html>

"Major General Alexander Hamilton." *Who Served Here? Historic Valley Forge.* n.d. <http://www.ushistory.org/valleyforge/served/hamilton.html>

Places to Visit

Federal Hall National Memorial
26 Wall Street
New York, New York 10005
(212) 825-6888
http://www.nps.gov/feha/

Hamilton Grange National Memorial
287 Convent Avenue
New York, New York 10005
(212) 666-1640
http://www.nps.gov/hagr/

Valley Forge National Historical Park
P.O. Box 953
Valley Forge, Pennsylvania 19482
(610) 783-1077
http://www.nps.gov/vafo/

Yorktown Battlefield Colonial National Historical Park
P.O. Box 210
Yorktown, Virginia 23690
(757) 898-2410
http://www.nps.gov/yonb/

Index